Understanding Asian Americans

A curriculum resource guide

Compiled and Edited by
Marjorie H. Li and Peter Li

Neal-Schuman Publishers
New York   London

Published by Neal-Schuman Publishers, Inc.
23 Leonard Street
New York, NY 10013

Printed and bound in the United States of America

Contributors
Joyce Penfield
Abraham Resnick
Penny W. Sing
Stella Ting-Toomey
Illustrations by   Margaret So

Library of Congress Cataloging-in-Publication Data

Understanding Asian Americans: a curriculum resource guide/compiled and edited by Marjorie H. Li and Peter Li.
p. cm.
Includes bibliographical references and index.
ISBN 1–55570–047–0
1. Asian Americans—Study and teaching (Elementary) I. Li. Marjorie H. II. Li, Peter, 1935-
E184.O6U5 1990
973'.0495'00712-dc20
    90–6670
    CIP

Dedicated to Pardee Lowe,
Mentor and Role Model

Contents

Preface   viii

Introduction, *Peter Li*   1

PART I: Perceptions of Asian Americans

Introduction: Stereotypes and Misperceptions, *Stella Ting-Toomey*   19
The Survey: Summary and Analysis, *Abraham Resnick*   23

PART II: Classroom Activities

Arts, Crafts, and Games, *Penny W. Sing*   33

1. Calligraphy   35
2. Carp kite   38
3. Chinese name chop or seal   40
4. New Year's parade   42
5. Chinese shuttlecock   45
6. Daruma Doll   47
7. Jan ken po   49
8. Haiku poetry   50
9. Origami   51
10. Paper cutting   53
11. Tangram   55
12. Khokad: Indian style tag   57
13. Alpana: Good luck designs   59
14. Games children play   61
15. What's in a name   62
16. Chopsticks Game   63

Understanding Cultural Diversity, *Joyce Penfield*   65

1. Asian Americans in literature   67
2. Careers   69
3. Media portrayal   70
4. "My image of . . . (name of country)"   72
5. Our stereotypes   73
6. Famous Asian Americans   75
7. "This is your life"—oral history   76
8. Family roles   77
9. Myths in history class   78
10. Film as catalyst   79
11. Cross-generational change   80
12. Geographic ethnocentrism   81
13. Tour guide   82
14. Self-awareness   83
15. Self-assessment   84
16. Stereotyping Americans   87

PART III: Recommendations to the Schools

Developing Resources, Broadening Perspectives, *Abraham Resnick*   91

Curriculum Improvement   93
Resources and Materials   93
Professional Initiatives   94
School-wide Programs and Events   95
Conclusion   95

PART IV: Annotated Bibliography

Introduction, *Marjorie H. Li* and *Peter Li*   99

Primary Level   101
Intermediate Level   108
Secondary Level   118
For General Readers: 125
  Asian and Asian Americans   125
  China and Chinese Americans   132
  India and Indian Americans   140
  Japan and Japanese Americans   144
  Other Asian Groups: Korea, The Philippines, Southeast Asia   151
  Ethnic Studies, Intercultural Relations, and General Reference
    Works   157

PART V: Appendixes and Index

Appendix A: Chronology of Asians in America   167
Appendix B: U.S. Legislation Regarding Asians   173
Appendix C: Survey Letter and Form: Perceptions of Asian
    Americans   177
Contributors   184
Index   185

Preface

The purpose of *Understanding Asian Americans: A Curriculum Resource Guide* is to provide information about Asia, Asians, and Asian Americans for a wide range of individuals—including teachers, principals, librarians, students, parents, community workers, and all who come into contact with Asian Americans or recent immigrants from Asia. Despite the 140-year history of Asians in America, Asians and Asian Americans are still not well understood in this country, and are often the victims of prejudice and discrimination. We believe that, by providing reliable information and finding the proper channel for its dissemination, we can reduce conflicts between ethnic and racial groups. We have compiled this volume to provide the most essential, up-to-date, practical, and reliable information available about Asians and Asian Americans.

Understanding Asian Americans offers an annotated bibliography, analytical essays, survey results, classroom activities, and suggestions to school administrators. The emphasis is on fostering as early as possible, a respect for cultural diversity and a sensitivity to cultural differences. We believe that the place to start cultivating these attitudes is in the schools. For this reason, the bibliography includes books and classroom activities appropriate for the primary school level.

The introduction discusses problems of cultural adjustment and establishment of a new identity. The adjustment period may be brief, or it may go on for several generations, depending on social and political conditions of the country and of the individuals themselves. The introduction also deals with the prospects for Asian Americans in the 1990s.

Part I summarizes the results of a survey on *Perceptions of Asian Americans* completed by both Asians and non-Asians. The central issues involved are stereotypes of Asian Americans, misconceptions regarding Asian Americans, and patterns of behavior within various Asian American groups. The survey questionnaires were distributed to the participants at the Sixth East Coast Asian American Education Conference (ECAAEC) held at Rutgers, The State University of New Jersey in New Brunswick, June 20–23, 1985. The results of this survey indicate how Asians feel about themselves and how non-Asians feel about Asians.

Part II presents 25 classroom activities for developing teacher and student sensitivity to interracial and intercultural problems. These activities are appropriate for various levels, some suitable for primary and intermediate level students, others for high school and college students, and some for all age groups (including adults). But it should be emphasized here that these activities, important as they are, are only as effective as the individual presenting them. Before conducting the activities the teacher or leader must frankly confront his or her own feelings regarding racial issues. This person must know his or her own prejudices and raise his or her own racial awareness.

Part III offers a list of suggestions for school officials and administrators. They are practical, concrete proposals that school authorities can put into effect to enrich the school curriculum, promote interracial and intercultural understanding, and add an international dimension to any school's curriculum.

Part IV contains selected annotated bibliographies of current works about Asians and Asian Americans. In addition to the more usual bibliographic entries on the arts, history, culture, and social studies, it includes works of fiction, poetry, short stories, and drama. Often a literary work presents a problem or issue better than a standard textbook. The materials are graded into four levels: primary (grades K-6), intermediate (grades 7–9), secondary (10–12), and those for the general reader. We have included as many new titles as possible. (The majority of the works were published within the last ten years.) Children's literature, such as folk tales, myths, and legends, on the primary and intermediate levels are included because we believe that education should begin at an early age.

Finally, we would like to acknowledge our thanks to the New Jersey Department of Higher Education for the Humanities Grant, which helped fund the Sixth East Coast Asian American Education Conference in June 1985; the International Center of Rutgers, the State University of New Jersey, which cosponsored the conference; the Pacific Asian Coalition (New Jersey Chapter) for a publications grant; the Chinese American Librarians Association and the Rutgers University Research Council for their grants-in-aid; and the New Jersey Ethnic Advisory Council for its support. A special thanks to Dr. C.S. Whitaker, Director of International Programs at Rutgers University, whose invaluable advice and support throughout this project made this book possible. Finally, a word of thanks to Steven Mark, who came on board in the final hours and made the book much more readable.

Peter Li

People must realize that there isn't such a thing as an Asian American. . . . There are Chinese, Koreans, Japanese, Vietnamese and so forth. So many different cultures. So many different experiences. We need to understand their differences and complexities, their successes and failures. The first priority for Americans is to learn more about Asia.

—*I.M. Pei*

Images do mold us. Blacks and athletics. Asians and academics. We've got to change the images.

—*Peter Wang*

The most pervasive worry among Asian Americans is that they have been typecast as superstars who achieve wonders in a few limited fields, particularly science and mathematics.

—*Robert B. Oxnam*

Introduction

Peter Li

ASIAN AMERICAN VOICES: IDENTITY AND DILEMMAS

Asian Americans have made significant contributions in many areas of American life, including science, technology, architecture, music, and art. One area that has recently reached maturity and has found a receptive audience is Asian American literature. David Henry Hwang's Broadway hit *M. Butterfly,* Maxine Kingston's *Woman Warrior,* and Amy Tan's *The Joy Luck Club* are some recent examples. These works have mass appeal not only because of their artistic merit but because they have introduced the general public to the sensibilities and experiences of Asians and Asian Americans in their relationships with the West.

I have chosen a number of selections from works by Asian American authors who have addressed questions of identity and acculturation. The materials are presented as a number of case studies: 1) self-rejection, 2) dual loyalty, 3) alienation, 4) generational conflict, 5) idealization of American life, 6) disillusionment, and 7) a new sensibility. These topics reflect the common concerns of many Asian Americans.

Case Study #1: Self-rejection

An immigrant settling in this country has to adjust to a new environment. Part of this adjustment process involves casting off old values, adopting new ones, and finding a new identity. Finding a new identity is a painful process, often involving not only rejection of old customs and habits but a total rejection of another self. In the last chapter of her autobiographical novel *The Woman Warrior*, Maxine Hong Kingston describes the feelings and actions of a 12- or 13-year-old Chinese American school girl when she comes face-to-face with another Chinese girl who is a newcomer to this country. Hate, anger, intolerance, and meanness emerge. Is it that she has found in the new girl a part of her former self? The new girl is variously called the "younger sister," the "quiet one," or "quiet sister." Kingston's novel has not pleased all its Asian American readers, but it is a powerful work.

> I hated the younger sister, the quiet one. I hated her when she was the last chosen for her team and I, the last chosen for my team. I hated her for her China doll haircut. I hated her at music time for the wheezes that came out of her plastic flute.
> One afternoon in the sixth grade, I and my little sister and the quiet girl and her big sister stayed late after school for some reason . . .
> I ran back into the girl's yard, and there was quiet sister all by herself. I ran past her, and she followed me into the girls' lavatory. My footsteps rang hard against the cement and tile because of the taps I had nailed into my shoes. Her footsteps were soft, padding after me. There was no one in the lavatory but the two of us. . . .
> I stopped abruptly in front of the sinks, and she came running toward me before she could stop herself, so that she almost collided with me. I walked closer. She backed away, puzzlement, then alarm in her eyes.
> "You're going to talk," I said, my voice steady and normal, as it is when talking to the familiar, the weak, and the small. "I'm going to make you talk, you sissy-girl." She stopped backing away and stood fixed.
> I looked into her face so I could hate it close up. She wore black bangs, and her cheeks were pink and white. She was baby-soft. . . .
> I reached up and took the fatty part of her cheek, not dough, but the meat between my thumb and finger . . . I gave her a face a squeeze. "Talk." When I let go, the pink rushed back into my white thumbprint on her skin. I walked around to her side. "Talk!" I shouted into the side of her head. Her straight hair hung, the same all these years, no ringlets or braids or permanents. I squeezed her other cheek. "Are you? Huh? Are you going to talk?"
> . . . She was so neat. Her neatness bothered me. I hated the way she folded the wax paper from her lunch; she did not wad her brown paper bag and her school papers. I hated her clothes . . .[1]

The protagonist calls her antagonist "the quiet one" because she does not speak. Through the eyes of this young school girl, we see the prejudice and critical intolerance of a second-generation Asian immigrant toward a first-generation arrival. The newcomer's looks, dress, and, above all, her silence and passivity disturb the protagonist. These characteristics seem to be all the more repugnant to the Chinese American girl because they remind her of the culture she is trying to leave behind.

Kingston has depicted a serious problem that plagues immigrants to this country: their inability to express themselves. Passages like these alert us to the fact that the inability to communicate is not only a barrier to understanding but also a source of pain and frustration that hinders the development of the individual.

Case Study #2: Dual Loyalty

Having been born and raised in one country and then uprooted to another with a different culture and tradition can be a trying experience. Aside from the issues of adjustment and acculturation, there is the problem of one's attachment to the old country. This is not easy to break, even with the best of intentions. The following passage from Jeanne Wakatsuki Houston's *Farewell to Manzanar* describes a poignant case of dual allegiance, in which the author's father is being detained and questioned by a United States government officer before being sent to an internment camp during World War II.

"What is your name?"
"Wakatsuki Ko."
"Your place of birth?"
"Ka-ke, a small town in Hiroshima-ken, on the island of Honshu."
"What schools did you attend in Japan?"
"Four years in Chuo Gakko, a school for training military officers."
"Why did you leave?"
"The marching. I got tired of the marching. That was not what I wanted to do."
. . .
"What do you think of the attack on Pearl Harbor?"
"I am sad for both countries. It is the kind of thing that always happens when military men are in control."
"What do you think of the American military? Would you object to your sons serving?"
"Yes. I would protest it. The American military is just like the Japanese."
"What do you mean?"
"They also want to make war when it is not necessary. As long as military men control the country you are always going to have war."
"Who do you think will win this one?"
"America, of course. It is richer, has more resources, more weapons, more people. The Japanese are courageous fighters, and they will fight well. But their leaders are stupid. I weep every night for my country."
"You say Japan is still your country?"

"I was born there. I still have relatives living there. In many ways, yes, it is still my country."

"Do you feel any loyalty to Japan or to its Emperor?"

Silence.

"I said, do you feel any loyalty . . .?"

"How old are you?"

"Twenty-nine."

"When were you born?"

"I am the interrogator here, Mr. Wakatsuki, not you."

"I am interested to know when you were born."

"Nineteen thirteen."

"I have been living in this country nine years longer than you have. Do you realize that? Yet I am prevented by law from becoming a citizen. I am prevented by law from owning land. I am now separated from my family without cause. . . ."

"Those matters are out of my hands, Mr. Wakatsuki."

"Whose hands are they in?"

"I do not like North Dakota any more than you do. The sooner we finish with these questions, the sooner we'll both be out of here."

"And where will you go when you leave?"

"Who do you want to win this war?"

"I am interested to know where you will be going when you leave?"

"Mr. Wakatsuki, if I have to repeat each one of these questions we will be here forever. Who do you want . . .?"

"When your mother and father are having a fight, do you want them to kill each other? Or do you just want them to stop fighting?"[2]

Mr. Wakatsuki has lived in the United States for more than 38 years, but has been prohibited by law from owning land and becoming a U.S. citizen. When war comes, he is uprooted from his home and family. Although he has lived in this country for a long time, he cannot help loving the country of his origin because he was born there and still has friends and relatives there.

In many cases, the immigrant is still deeply attached to his or her homeland, despite an equally strong tie to the adopted country. Therefore, when war breaks out between the two "homelands" it is like fighting within the family. The new immigrant does not pray for either side to win or lose, only for the fighting to end.

Case Study #3: Alienation

Related to the previous case study is the case of a second-generation Japanese American (nisei) who is sent to an internment camp, where he is asked to swear allegiance to the U.S. government. When he refuses, he is sent to prison for two years. After his release, he finds that his world—and he himself—has changed. The passage is from John Okada's novel *No-No Boy:*

> There was a time when I was your son. There was a time that I no longer remember when you used to smile a mother's smile and tell me stories about gallant and fierce warriors who protected their lords with blades of shining steel and about old woman who found a peach in the stream and took it home, and, when her husband split it in half, a husky little boy tumbled out to fill their hearts with boundless joy.
>
> I was that lad in the peach and you were the old woman and we were Japanese with Japanese feelings, and Japanese pride and Japanese thoughts because it was all right then to be Japanese and feel and think all the things that Japanese do even if we lived in America.
>
> Then there came a time when I was only half Japanese because one is not born in America and raised in America and taught in America and one does not speak and swear and drink and smoke and play and fight and see and hear in America among Americans in American streets and houses without becoming American and loving it.
>
> But I did not love enough, for you were still half my mother and I was thereby still half Japanese and when the war came and they told me to fight for America, I was not strong enough to fight the bitterness which made the half of me which was you bigger than the half of me that I could not see or feel. Now that I know the truth when it is late and the half of me which was you is no longer there, I am only half of me and the half that remains is American by law because the government was wise and strong enough to know why it was that I could not fight for America and did not strip me of my birthright. But it is not enough to be only half American and know that it is an empty half. I am not your son and I am not Japanese and I am not American.[3]

The protagonist, Ichiro, finds himself totally cut off from his world. His experience is traumatic. He is no longer Japanese, no longer American, and no longer even his mother's son. His friends spit on him. He is rejected by his own people, and he is not accepted by Americans. Because he cannot accept the Japan of his parents, he cannot identify with them any longer and be their child. Only after shedding the Japanese part of himself can Ichiro begin his search for a new identity.

Case Study #4: Generational Conflict

The following passage is about a second-generation Chinese American girl rebelling against her parents, trying to assert her independence and individuality. The passage is from Jade Snow Wong's 1950 best-sell-ing novel *Fifth Chinese Daughter*. Jade Snow is about to go on a date with her Chinese American boyfriend, Joe. Her parents object to her going out unchaperoned. Jade Snow tells her parents calmly:

> "This is something you should think more about now. I am too old to whip and I am too old to be treated as a child. I can think for myself, and you and Mama should not demand unquestioning obedience from me. You should understand me. There was a time in America when parents raised children to make them work, but now the foreigners regard them as individuals with rights of their own. I have worked too, but now I am an individual, besides being your fifth daughter."
>
> Astounded by his daughter's audacity, her father argues: "What would happen to the order of this household if each of our four children started to behave like individuals? Would we have one peaceful moment if your personal desires came before your duty? How could we maintain our self-respect if we, your parents did not know where you were at night and with whom you were keeping company?"
>
> Her mother adds: "Of course, we will not permit you to run the risk of corrupting your purity before marriage."
>
> To which Jade Snow retorts: "Oh Mama! This is America not China. Don't you think I have any judgment? How can you think I would go out with just any man? Both of you should understand that I am growing up to be a woman in a society greatly different from the one you knew in China. You expect me to work my way through college—which would not have been possible in China. . . . Of course, independence is not safe. But safety isn't the only consideration. You must give me the freedom to find some answers for myself."
>
> Her father, the product of only one culture, can only reply in terms he knows. He tells her pointedly: "You are shameless. Your skin is yellow. Your features are forever Chinese. We are content with proven ways. Do not try to force foreign ideas into my home. Go! You will one day tell us sorrowfully that you have been mistaken."[4]

The generational conflict depicted here is part of the acculturation process of second-generation Asian immigrants whose cultural values begin to differ from those of their parents'. The parents and children no longer see things eye-to-eye. The parents still adhere to the values of the country of their origin, but the children, having been raised and educated in America, adopt the values of their new homeland. The conflict here brings out such issues as an adolescent's desire for freedom, challenge to parental authority, and harmony within the family.

The reprimand by the father at the end of the passage would have been unbearable in the old country. But in America, the girl will simply continue leading her own life, going to school or work. However, as is usually the case in generational conflicts in the new country, the parents eventually give in, realizing that the times have changed.

Case Study #5: The Idealization Of America

Although Filipino immigrant Carlos Bulosan experienced much frustration and disappointment after coming to America, he wrote with the courage and idealism that motivates many new U.S. immigrants. Bulosan also strove to speak for the many agricultural workers and industrial laborers of America, and to give them hope. This passage is from Bulosan's autobiographical work of 1947, *America   Is in the Heart:*

> America is not a land of one race or one class of men. We are all Americans that have toiled and suffered and known oppression and defeat, from the first Indian that offered peace in Manhattan to the last Filipino peapicker.
> America is not bound by geographical latitudes.
> America is not merely a land or an institution.
> America is in the hearts of men that died for freedom; it is also in the eyes of men that are building a new world. America is a prophecy of a new society of men: of a system that knows no sorrow or strife or suffering. America is a warning to those who would try to falsify the ideals of free men.
> America is also the nameless foreigner, the homeless refugee, the hungry boy begging for a job and the black body dangling from a tree. America is the illiterate immigrant who is ashamed that the world of books and intellectual opportunities is closed to him. We are all that nameless foreigner, that homeless refugee, that hungry boy, that illiterate immigrant and that lynched black body. All of us from the first Adams to the last Filipino, native born or alien, educated or illiterate—we are America.[5]

Despite his seeming optimism and exhilaration, Carlos Bulosan suffered severe loneliness and depression. His love of America and the expression of courage and hope were part of his effort to set down roots in his new homeland. Although Bulosan became a celebrated writer, especially in the 1940s, he was never able to achieve his dream of improving the life of migrant Filipino workers.

Case Study #6: Disillusionment

While Carlos Bulosan's sense of hope and inspiration comes from a conscious attempt to win sympathy and support for the suffering workers in Asian America, Pardee Lowe's *Father and Glorious Descendant*

documents the harsh realities of an innocent Chinese boy's first attempt
to find a job in the racially sensitive California of 1918:

> During this period my youthful cup of patriotism was filled to over-
> flowing. In the first place our Americanism had finally reached the ears of
> the White House. The christening of my twin brothers brought two impor-
> tant letters of congratulation from Washington, . . . Vice President Marshall's
> letter to father . . . was a human one, glowing with warmth and inspiration.
> There was one sentence which stood out: "To be a good American citizen,
> in my judgment, is about the best thing on earth, and while I cannot endow
> your children with any worldly goods, I can bless them with the hope that
> they may grow up to be an honor to their parents and a credit to the
> commonwealth. . . ."
>
> The next summer, my thirteenth, I decided to go to work during
> vacation. I needed spending money badly for my first term in high school.
> Father applauded this show of independence until I informed him that I
> intended, if possible, to become an office boy in an American business firm.
> They he was seized with profound misgivings. "Would they hire you?"
> father inquired.
>
> "Why won't they," I replied, with overweening self-confidence. "See!" I
> pointed to the Sunday edition of the *San Francisco Chronicle*. "I can hold any
> of these jobs." . . . Blithely one sunny July morning I set forth job hunting, .
> . .
>
> Opening a door marked PRIVATE, the girl announced, "Mr. Royal, here
> is another boy." He raised his head. . . . "Young man," he said, "I understand
> you would like to work for us? Well then you'd better tell us something of
> yourself."
>
> "Why, of course," I said, "of course." And impulsively I told everything:
> all about my graduation from grammar school, my boy-scout training, and
> my desire to earn my own keep during the summer.
>
> Mr. Royal seemed visibly impressed. When a faint smile replaced his
> frown, I stopped fidgeting. I fully expected him to ask me to come to work
> in the morning. Therefore, I was appalled when he told me that he was sorry,
> but all the jobs were taken. It never occurred to me that our interview would
> end like this.[6]

This early disappointment was to leave a lasting impression on
young Pardee Lowe. He soon realized that his youthful dream of America as the land of opportunity, where anyone can become the President
of the United States, was unfounded. Later young Pardee was to learn
that the job that the manager said was already "taken" continued to be
advertised for weeks in the newspapers. For an Asian boy, looking for a
summer job became a poignant lesson in race relations. In spite of
disappointments, however, Pardee Lowe persisted in his efforts to fulfill

himself and to find his niche in his new homeland. If he cannot fulfill his dream to the fullest, perhaps his son will.

Case Study #7: A New Sensibility

Since the late 1960s, a new generation of Asian American writers has developed a voice in Asian American literature. An angry generation that looks askance at the tradition and culture of the old country, they are constructing their own identity and striving for a new sensibility. Having rejected their roots, they must find new ones. In his recent play *The Chickencoop Chinaman*, Frank Chin proposes one answer. It should be noted here that Chin's use of the term "Chinaman" is a deliberate flouting of tradition. It is calculated to raise eyebrows.

> Girl: Where were you born?
> Tam: Chinamen are made, not born, my dear. Out of junk imports, lies, railroad scrap iron, dirty jokes, broken bottles, cigar smoke, Cosquilla Indian blood, wino spit, and lots of milk amnesia.
> Girl: You sure have a way with words. . . . and then you were born?
> Tam: (As a Bible Belt Preacher) Born? No! Crashed! Not born. Stamped! Not born! Created! Not born. No more born than the heaven and earth. No more born than nylon or acrylic. For I am a Chinaman! A miracle synthetic. Drip dry and machine washable. For now in one point of time and space, as never before and never after, in this one instant of eternity, was focused that terrific, that awesome power of the universe that marks a moment divine. . . .[7]

By rejecting its attachment to the old homeland, the new generation of Chinese American writer must establish an identity of its own. The new Asian American, the "Chinaman," is like "a miracle synthetic," something artificially made, not born. Have they succeeded? It is too early to tell. Their voice is a troubled one. There is a swagger to their manner. Are they trying to restore masculinity to the male ego, emasculated in the new culture where women have often adjusted more quickly than men? The answer remains to be seen.

Some of the writers are first-generation, some second-generation, and others third- or fourth-generation Asian Americans, but they are still searching for their identity. Assimilation or acculturation is not necessarily a matter of one generation; it may go on for several generations. Each generation must find its own solution. Each writer is at a different stage of his or her search for an identity. The following may be helpful in understanding the process of acculturation.

The first generation of an immigrant group experiences cultural shock, disorganization as the immigrants leave their old homeland and settle in the new country. Their first concern is sheer survival. However, after they have experienced some degree of success and their children have become acculturated by attending school and interacting with other children, they begin to fear that their own culture, language, customs, and beliefs are going to be lost. As a result, a second phase occurs in which the native traditions and culture are self-consciously preserved. In the third phase, the group develops a sense of pride, even though it acknowledges and submits to the white Anglo majority. However, it does now harbor a degree of antagonism and resentment. In the fourth stage there emerges a strident militancy. The group feels that it is as good as any other group. It need not acquiesce to others. By now the group has become solidly middle class and moves toward the upper middle class.[8]

In the fifth phase, militancy changes to self-hate and anti-militancy. As members of the group become upper middle class and professional, secure in their positions, they have the leisure to reflect on and re-evaluate circumstances. Latent self-rejection and self-criticism come to the forefront. The group becomes critical of its traditions, finding them limiting and repugnant, but at the same time not wanting to abandon them completely. In the final stage, the group finds comfort and security in its cultural heritage. The members no longer feel ashamed. In fact they have a strong interest in finding their roots in the old country. The younger generation, especially, will go on trips to the old country to find out how their ancestors lived.

PROGRAM FOR THE 1990s

In the 140-year history of Asians in America, Asians and Asian Americans have suffered the most vicious forms of racial discrimination, from legal exclusion and mob violence to the government-sanctioned internment of over 100,000 Americans of Japanese descent. However, despite a string of hardships and setbacks, Asian immigrants today enter the United States at a higher rate than every before. And there are positive signs. Whereas 100 years ago California was a hotbed of anti-Asian violence and discrimination, today Asians find California one of the most desirable places to live.

What is in store for Asian Americans in the next decade? Let us turn to some statistics. At the present time, there are about five million

Americans of Asian descent, making up 1.8 percent of the total population of the United States. But although Asian Americans comprise only
a small part of the population, their influence has been far greater than
their numbers would suggest. The architectural landscape of America
has been changed by Asian American architects I.M. Pei and Yoshiro
Yamasaki. The musical world is studded with names like Seiji Ozawa,
Yo Yo Ma, Kyung-Wha Chung, and Zubin Mehta. An Wang created one
of the nation's largest computer companies, and Benihana's Rocky Aoki
founded one of the largest restaurant chains in the country. Samuel Ting
was awarded a Nobel Prize in physics. In New York City, Korean
Americans run 56 percent of the 1,600 green groceries in the city. Filipino
doctors now outnumber African American doctors and have become
general practitioners in many rural communities that once lacked phy-
sicians. On the West coast, Asian Indians own 800 of the some 6,000
motels in California. In parts of Texas, the Vietnamese control 85 percent
of the shrimp fishing industry. In almost every conceivable field, Asian
Americans have made significant contributions.[9] Asian Americans' ac-
complishments can be virtually unlimited. It is up to them to decide their
future.

In the past, Asian Americans have shied away from politics and
community activities. As a result of the civil rights movement of the
1960s, however, a new Asian American political and social consciousness has evolved. This has led to active participation in politics—running for political office, accepting appointments to official positions, and
participating in community affairs, including local school boards. More
and more Asian Americans are now actively involved in politics and
government.[10]

Because of their appearance, Asian Americans will often be mistaken
for foreigners or newcomers by the mainstream Anglo population.
However, when new friends come up to compliment a politically or
socially involved Asian American with "Oh, you speak English very
well!" or "Where are you from?" they need not feel offended. In fact, in
our ethnically conscious society today, ethnicity and diversity may be
assets rather than handicaps.

There are, of course, more important reasons for becoming actively
involved in politics and community affairs. Foremost is to protect and
fight for the rights and privileges that legitimately belong to Asian
Americans. An issue that has recently emerged in the news media is
whether there is an unwritten admissions quota for Asian Americans at
prestigious universities in the country today.[11] Many Asian Americans
immediately formed investigative committees to gather facts and apply

pressure on the universities to disclose their admissions criteria. If there is a quota system, then the groups can decide on legal action.

Another issue that needs to be addressed by Asian Americans is the recent media blitz about Asian Americans being the "model minority."[12] It is, of course, flattering to be praised. And to have risen "from pariahs to paragons"[13] in the hundred years from the 1880s to the 1980s is surely no mean feat. But the "model minority" image is only a half truth and obscures many deep-seated problems in the Asian American community. The academically and financially successful constitute a small minority. The handful of Asian Americans who have made it are in the limelight; there are many who have failed—but they go unnoticed. A casual walk through many Asian American communities in urban centers will reveal substandard housing and a poor working environment. Many people need help to obtain adequate housing, medical care, and instruction in English and other academic areas.

The high average income of Asian American families has also been noted in the press, but not much attention has been given to the fact that this is not due to the breadwinners earning high salaries, but because more household members are employed, often working long hours. The educational level of Asian Americans again is generally higher than the national average, but few seem to be able to use that advantage as a springboard to managerial positions. Asian Americans continue to earn considerably less than their white counterparts. Subtle forms of discrimination, institutional, personal, and societal, exist at various levels in the social hierarchy. These facts must be pointed out and addressed by the united, organized voice of Asian Americans.

As we edge closer to the twenty-first century, it is becoming clear that Asia—especially the Pacific rim countries—has emerged into economic prominence. This has forced mainstream American society to look with greater interest at the language, culture, and history of Asian countries. These subjects have become popular in schools and universities.[14] Many Asian Americans who once rejected or neglected their own cultural heritage are taking an active interest in it. Now there are economic advantages in being bilingual and bicultural, aside from the psychological and social benefits. As interaction between East and West increases, the bicultural Asian American will be playing a more important role in bridging the cultural and communication gaps.

Striding tentatively into its third century, American society faces serious social, economic, and political challenges in the areas of productivity, high technology, substance abuse, the strength of the dollar, and international relations. What has gone wrong? What are the solutions to these problems? Perhaps we can find answers to some of these problems in the cultural values and belief system of Asian countries. The Confucian work ethic and Japanese management system have helped Asian countries gain the economic edge. The emphasis placed on education has helped many Asians in this country take full advantage of the educational opportunities. Although devising action plans from cross-cultural comparisons is fraught with peril, it is possible to examine some indications. For example, recent comparative studies of educational systems between Asian countries and America may lead to long-range educational reforms in this country.[15] In the final analysis, being an Asian American may not be so bad after all. As a young Chinese American once said:

> I remember telling him [father] that I was an American first and that being Chinese wasn't so hot. He said that one day, I'm going to want to know everything there is to know about being Chinese, and I thought he was just crazy and that was one of his old-fashioned ideas. But it was true, eventually that need was there in me—a craving to know more about myself after so many years of self-denial about being Chinese and Asian.[16]

Finally, it may be legitimate to ask: Who are the Asian Americans? What do they have in common? Do they have a common culture, language, tradition that help identify them? Or are they an amorphous group that defies definition? There are no simple answers to these questions. Asian Americans form a diverse group with different religious, linguistic, cultural, and political backgrounds. While understanding this complex group does present a challenge, the resulting enhanced communication and insight benefit not only Asian Americans, but each group that helps form the intricate tapestry of America's cultural heritage.

NOTES

1. Maxine Hong Kingston, *The Woman Warrior: Memoirs of a Girlhood Among Ghosts* (New York: Vintage Books, 1976), 201–205.
2. Jeanne Wakatsuki Houston, *Farewell to Manzanar* (Boston: Houghton Mifflin, 1973), 43–46.
3. John Okada, *No-No Boy* (Seattle: University of Washington Press, 1976 [1957]), 15–16.
4. Jade Snow Wong, *Fifth Chinese Daughter* (New York: Harper & Row, 1950), 128–30; also see *Asian-American Authors* (Boston: Houghton Mifflin, 1972), edited by Kai-yu Hsu and Helen Palubinskas, 19–22.

5. Carlos Bulosan, *America Is in the Heart* (Seattle: University of Washington Press, 1943), 189.
6. Pardee Lowe, Jr., *Father and Glorious Descendant* (Little, Brown, 1943, 1971), 142-46; also see *Asian-American Authors,* 19–22.
7. Frank Chin, *The ChickenCoop Chinaman and The Year of the Dragon* (Seattle: University of Washington Press, 1981), 6–8.
8. Andrew M. Greeley, *Why Can't They Be Like Us? America's White Ethnic Groups* (New York: E.P. Dutton, 1971), 53–59.
9. David A. Bell, "The Triumph of Asian Americans," *The New Republic* (July 15 and 22, 1985): 24–31. Robert Oxnam, "Why Asians Succeed Here," *New York Times Magazine* (Nov. 30, 1986). Two informative recent articles on Asian Americans that provide much valuable data.
10. See Farland Chang's unpublished master's project at Columbia University's School of Journalism, "Chinese Americans in American Politics," in which he followed the campaigns of two recent candidates for political office: S.B. Woo, a physics professor at the University of Delaware, and Peter Ng, a New York real estate broker. There are, of course, numerous others who are already in office, such as Daniel K. Inouye, senator from Hawaii, and March Fong Eue, the three-term secretary of state of California.
11. Lawrence Biemiller, "Asian Students Fear Top Colleges Use Quota System," *The Chronicle of Higher Education* XXXIII, 12 (Nov. 19, 1986). The allegations are that Asians and Asian American students are applying in large numbers—sometimes twice or three times the number of previous applicants—to elite colleges and universities, but the numbers admitted have not kept up with the increase in applications. "Bunzel: Institutional Practices Block Asians' College Admissions," *Asianweek* 8, 39 (May 15, 1987). One of the claims here is that Asians have to score 112 points higher than Caucasians on the SAT to gain admission to Harvard.
12. The idea of the Asian American "model minority" began to gain popularity in the latter half of the 1960s with an article in the *New York Times Magazine* (January 1966) and *U.S. News and World Report* (December 1966) and has snowballed since in the 1970s and 1980s. The recent articles by David A. Bell and Robert Oxnam (see footnote 10) attempt to find the reasons Asians have succeeded so well here.
13. Peter I. Rose, "Asian Americans: From Pariahs to Paragons," *Clamor at the Gates,* ed. Nathan Glazer (San Francisco: ICS Press, 1985), 181–212.
14. Ronald Takaki, *Strangers from a Different Shore* (Boston: Little Brown & Co., 1989), 475–77.
15. I have not seen statistics on this yet, but informal talks with colleagues suggest an increased enrollment across the country in Chinese and Japanese language classes and generally in history and economics classes dealing with Asia.
16. Harold Stevenson, "Making the Grade: School Achievement in Japan, Taiwan, and the United States," *Center for Advanced Study in the Behavioral Sciences Annual Report 1983:* 41–51. Professor Stevenson headed a large-scale comparative investigation into the educational practices, educational atti-

tudes of parents and teachers in China, Japan, and the United States. The results show that parental attitudes and expectations were important as well as the amount of time spent in school and on homework. It was not believed that the students in any group were smarter than the others. The conclusion was that hard work made the difference.

Part I

Perceptions of Asian Americans

Introduction: Stereotypes and Misperceptions

Stella Ting-Toomey

We all hold multidimensional images about ourselves, about others, and about members of entire social or cultural groups. Sometimes these images correspond to reality; at other times, they do not. But our tendency to categorize and to form impressions of groups of people in their social environment based on these images is a natural part of the cognitive process. Although this subjective categorization gives the perceiver a sense of order, stability, and control, it may not always be accurate.

We frequently act upon our subjective perceptions as if they were real. We behave and react toward another individual on the basis of our impressions and, in the context of intercultural communication, on the basis of cultural stereotypes. We stereotype tall people, short people, occupational groups, males and females, African Americans, Hispanics, Native Americans—and Asian Americans are no exception. Although stereotyping is a natural process of learning, cultural stereotypes have a profound impact on our communication with people from another culture. To the extent that our stereotypes are "positive" toward an individual from that culture, we may tend to be hospitable toward that individual. If our stereotypes are "negative," then we may act with hostility or aggressiveness. To the degree that our stereotypes are open and flexible, we allow our actual interaction experience with this individual to be our guide. To the extent that our stereotypes are closed and rigid, we let our preconceived notions dictate our behavior and our judgments.

Values

Aside from perceptions and stereotypes, our behavior is strongly influenced by fundamental cultural values. These values, which bind and systematize our diffuse perceptions of reality into a coherent design, refer to a set of beliefs that guide our actions and thoughts and give us our sociocultural identity. They influence our motivations, expectations, and behavioral reactions toward other individuals. Our communication with members of another ethnic or cultural group is guided implicitly by our set of psychological, social, and cultural values. In comparing the United States, Greece, India, and Japan, researchers found that in the United States self-confidence, individual achievement, and good adjustment are highly valued, whereas in Greece, affiliation, societal well-being, and *philotimos* (obeying the norms of the culture) are most valued. In India, increased status, glory, and societal well-being are treasured; and in Japan, serenity, esthetic satisfaction, and contentment are highly regarded ideals.[1] We see that each cultural group has selected a set of values peculiar to themselves. Therefore, in order to promote better understanding among people from different cultures, we need to look into our stereotypical perceptions, value systems, and patterns of communication. Where do our stereotypes come from? How do values influence our communication? Finally, what should we do to promote better relations among the various cultural groups in the United States?

The Survey

To find answers to the above questions, the authors of this book developed a survey on "Perceptions of Asian Americans" (see Appendix C). The survey was distributed to approximately 150 participants at the Sixth East Coast Asian American Education Conference, held at Rutgers, The State University of New Jersey in June 1985. The rate of return was about 25 percent. (We hope that readers will turn to Appendix C at the back of this book and fill in and return the survey to the editors so that our research can be continued.) The participants of the conference were predominantly Asians, with Chinese Americans in the majority, followed by Japanese Americans, and, finally, Korean Americans and Asian Indians.

The survey was made up of three parts: Part I had general questions on stereotypes and misperceptions; Part II asked questions on values and communication patterns; and Part III solicited constructive suggestions for Asian American studies in the schools.

Some of the significant findings of the survey were:

1. "inscrutability" is still regarded as one of the three most common stereotypes about Asian Americans, along with industriousness and intelligence;
2. passivity and unassertiveness are regarded as the most serious misperceptions about Asian Americans;
3. the sources of the stereotypes are the media, films, and books;
4. these misperceptions can be corrected by teaching Asian history in the schools and by a concerted public relations campaign;
5. almost all the respondents believe that Asian languages should be taught in the schools;
6. ideally, the Asian studies teacher should be open-minded, sensitive, and empathetic toward Asian Americans. It would be good, also, if he or she is bilingual and has traveled in Asia. But the teacher does not have to be an Asian American.

NOTE

1. Harry Tirandis, et al. *The Analysis of Subjective Culture* (New York: Wiley, 1972).

The Survey
Analysis and Summary

Abraham Resnick

The first question on our survey form is: *What do you think are the three most common stereotypes non-Asians have concerning Asian Americans?* The most common answers we have received so far are: they are industrious, intelligent, and demonstrate inscrutability. The respondents also included such characteristics as shyness, humility, obedience, submissiveness, family orientation, respect for elders, and clannish nature. They felt that Asian Americans were also goal-oriented, set high standards for themselves and their families, and place high value on the benefit of education. The latter characteristic was often mentioned in association with their exceptional skills in mathematics and science. They were thought by non-Asians to be good business people, specializing in owning restaurants and laundries. Competitiveness and concern with affluence and upward mobility were singled out, along with an attitude of willingness to make concessions, to compromise, and to sacrifice for the good of the group.

A number of negative connotations were also identified, including such descriptions as distant, untrustworthy, cunning, crafty, and sneaky.

Some respondents thought that non-Asians view Asians as foreigners, displaced persons from war zones, people unable to speak English, with "exotic traits." One person thought non-Asians view Asian women as sex objects.

2. *What do you think are the sources of these stereotypes?* The most frequently mentioned sources of stereotypes were the media, films (es-

pecially older movies), and books. A broad array of other contributing factors were enumerated. They included such items as basic racist assumptions, hearsay information, superficial knowledge, lack of cultural and historical perspective, dearth of curriculum materials about Asians, and deep-rooted ethnocentrism on the part of non-Asian Americans.

Additional factors included: the limited exposure of non-Asians to Asians, jealousy over their rapid advancement in the United States, the language barrier, threat of Japanese goods taking over American markets, travel or military experiences in Asia, cultural and physical disparities, and what is viewed as the mysterious, isolated nature of Asian enclaves.

possible non-verbal hindrances in communication

3. *What do you think are the three most serious misperceptions non-Asians have concerning Asian Americans?* The most conspicuous and most serious misperceptions of Asians held by non-Asians, according to the respondents, are that Asians are inclined to be passive or unassertive, tend to be inscrutable, and are of a common culture, having a uniform ethnicity.

Other answers to this item included such generalized comments as: all Asians are alike; they are all successful; Asians are more Asian than American; they are clannish; they will tolerate much abuse and denial of their rights, are unable to communicate in English, take jobs away from Americans, are slow to assimilate, rely on the extended family to resolve their own problems, are unreliable in international relations. On the other hand, Asians are also seen as a model minority.

4. *Do you have any specific suggestions as to how these misperceptions can be corrected?* The respondents advanced a number of suggestions for correcting misperceptions about Asians. Most felt that more stress and attention should be given to Asian studies in the schools. It was assumed that the promotion of better educational programs, more valid coverage of Asian topics in textbooks, and the availability of curriculum materials and themes for workshops about Asians would prove beneficial.

Other recommended strategies were: the organization of a unified public relations campaign that would establish community and political action and advocacy groups, direct an appeal to the media to be more sensitive to Asian issues, and become more active in speaking out on glaring and persistent misperceptions.

The second part of the survey explored values and communication patterns. Respondents were asked to choose one specific Asian American ethnic group they are familiar with to answer these questions:

1. *What do you think are the three most important core cultural values of this particular Asian American group (Chinese, Japanese, Korean, Filipino, or Vietnamese)?* The compilation and synthesis of the responses of each of

the above Asian American groups demonstrated marked similarity in identifying important core cultural values.

The three most prevalent values listed were: strong support of and loyalty to the family; great emphasis on achievement, especially in academic pursuits; and the premium put on the work ethic. Other core cultural values cited were: patience and endurance; humility; hospitality and politeness; quietness; compliance with parental expectations; cultural identity and commitment; concern with image (face); obedience and respect for authority; capacity for denial and willingness to defer and sacrifice; and respect for elders.

2. What would be the key phrases or adjectives that best describe this particular Asian American group in their interaction with other non-Asian groups? For the interactions of the Chinese community with non-Asian groups, descriptive words such as timid, withdrawn, isolated, passive, submissive, avoidance, noninvolved, and unassertive were given. Other descriptions appeared to be contradictory, such as curious, apologetic, distrustful, generous, cautious, chauvinistic, low-key, uptight, unsociable, and superior.

The Japanese interaction process was viewed as being respectful, tentative, cautious, curious, spartan, stoic, and deferential.

The Koreans were seen as competitive, having low esteem of self and group in the American socialization process, and facing dissension within ranks.

The Filipinos described themselves as outspoken, uniform, and having the capacity to assimilate easily.

The Vietnamese people were thought to be cooperative, knowledgeable, and assertive in their human relationships.

3. Do you feel there is a major communication style difference between this particular Asian American group and non-Asian groups? There was an 87.5 percent "yes" response for Chinese Americans. The answers for the Japanese was 50 percent "yes" and 50 percent "little difference." For Filipinos, it was 67 percent "yes." For Vietnamese and Korean groups, it was 100% yes. By far, the overwhelming number of responses for this item were from the Chinese Americans. The remaining responses were considerably fewer and may be seen as statistically insignificant.

Many respondents elected not to contribute explanations to this inquiry; others were vague and inconclusive. Reasons given for the large difference in communication style for the Chinese included that they were: less expressive and less inclined to take the initiative, willing to compromise and to show tolerance, exhibit an unassertive, quiet manner, are uncomfortable with non-Chinese, have and place a premium on silence. The Japanese, it was said, develop a good rapport before doing business and are greatly concerned with image and with the impact of statements made. The Koreans, it was claimed, place a stress on their cultural values, which avoid candid, confrontational communication. Respect for others is essential. This view was echoed as a Filipino trait as well. The Vietnamese response noted the war in Southeast Asia as a major factor in the ways they interact with other groups.

4. *If you are in contact with members of this particular Asian American group on a regular basis, can you recall an incident from the recent past that has caused communication breakdown or conflict between a member of this particular Asian American group and the other person (or yourself)?* There were no responses to this question.

5. *Are there recent problems in Asian American communities which you feel need to be identified and addressed?* Again there were no responses to this question. There may be a reluctance on the part of the participants to focus on unpleasant incidents during the conference.

6. *What problems do Asian American children have in adjusting to life in the United States (e.g., first-generation parents vs. second-generation children?* A number of problems were singled out. They included negative name calling by other Americans; peer pressure to quickly assimilate and become "Americanized"; language and cultural differences with Americans, parents, and older community members; resolving filial devotion expectations to parents; intra- and inter-cultural dating practices; pressure by parents to excel in school and succeed on the job; not being fully accepted by Americans, compounded by racial and self-image dilemmas on self-hatred and inferiority. Other factors noted in the adjustment problem were a feeling of displacement, lack of understanding on the part of educators, sense of isolation and social rejection, and authoritative and overly protective parents.

7. *Name some ways in which the adjustment of these Asian American children affect family life?* Ways in which adjustments of Asian American children affect family life include: teenage rebellion, which fosters a generation gap, family tensions and anxieties over competing loyalties, separation and alienation from family, communication breakdowns, role reversals, guilt feelings, and fear and insecurity.

8. *What do you perceive as the major intercultural communication problems that face members of this particular group when communicating with non-Asians?* The answers to this question underline that barriers in communication between groups do indeed exist. The major difficulties were viewed as stemming from prejudice, racism, negative stereotypes, misperceptions, lack of understanding, cultural disparities, societal pat-

communication problems

terns relating to sex and intermarriage, lack of sensitivity, socioeconomic class differences, jealousy, fear of competition and job loss, language barrier, ethnocentricity, both superiority and inferiority complexes, and Asian identification with whites rather than blacks.

9. *What do you perceive as the major intercultural communication problems that face members of this particular group when communicating with members of other Asian groups?* Based on the reasons given, a large measure of intra-Asian communication disharmony can be attributed to the language barrier, prejudices learned in the "old country," lack of social opportunities for mixing, inertia of leaders, use of own cultural values as the acceptable norm, hard feelings and hatred, vanity, competition, lack of patience and tolerance, and perception of one's own social status as being higher than other groups.

10. *If a curriculum handbook for teachers were developed, what key terms would you include in the glossary that would be helpful for understanding Asian Americans?* Many of the terms and key vocabulary cited in the aforementioned responses were recommended again for inclusion in a curriculum handbook to be used by teachers.

The third section of the survey considered the instructional setting.

1. *If you were to implement the ideal Asian American course in the school curriculum for the purpose of understanding Asian American experiences and cultures, what would be some of the key topics you would include?* Based on the consensus derived from the survey, there is a general agreement that there needs to be a greater emphasis placed on the study of Asian history, especially as it relates to American history, in the curriculum of U.S. schools. There was also a recognition that topics such as Asian immigration, differences and similarities among the cultures of various Asian groups, and their comparisons to the American culture pattern should be treated in the schools. Other topics included: geography, racism, creative arts, philosophies, and contemporary affairs. A number of respondents recommended that a case study approach be used in the instructional process.

teaching strategies

2. *Can you suggest some specific activities that have worked well in your experience?* A broad array of teaching methods were suggested, including inquiry and panel discussions, case studies, guest speakers, films and assigned viewing of television documentaries, involvement in student exchange programs, theater productions and variety shows, social events, involvement in UNICEF activities, historical fiction, and oral and written reporting.

3. *What do you think should be the ideal characteristics or qualities of an instructor who teachers such a course?* The most pronounced trait required

for teaching a course about Asian Americans was the need for the instructor to be open-minded, sensitive, and empathetic toward the Asian American experience. Beyond that, it was regarded as imperative that the teacher possess fine teaching and communications skills, be committed, know the issues and culture, have a broad general background about Asian Americans, have contact with Asian Americans, and, preferably, be Asian American. It was also suggested that the teacher be bilingual and have travel experience in Asia.

4. *What do you think should be the ideal background experiences of such an instructor?* The ideal background noted paralleled the essential criteria given in the previous question (see III. C.), with the additional suggestion that the instructor have a background in psychology, in an Asian language, and familiarity with Asian philosophies and religions.

5. *If you are a teacher/instructor or Asian American professional involved with Asian American activities, would you like to receive additional training to deal more effectively with Asian Americans? No Yes . If yes, what kind of training would you like to receive?* Participants in the study who indicated "yes" suggested the following kinds of additional training: courses in language, history, civilization, comparative cultures, race relations, workshops in counseling Asian Americans, field study in an Asian country, and a seminar in methods for dealing with Asians.

6. *Recommendations.* Respondents were asked to recommend helpful resources.

7. *What recommendations do you have for improving understanding Asian Americans for which the schools can take special responsibility?* Recommendations included: increase the number of courses offered in the curriculum about Asian American subjects; improve the social studies program in the schools by placing more emphasis on Asian values, history, geography and current events; recruit better guidance counselors, familiar with Asian students and their problems; encourage Asian parents to become involved in school support associations like the PTA; and adopt textbooks that provide greater coverage of Asian topics. Furthermore, it was thought that Asian American relations could be advanced in the schools by having libraries subscribe to Asian American newspapers, journals, and resources, by establishing Asian American speakers bureaus, by recognizing an Asian theme or celebration for study and commemoration, by having more Asian faculty, by encouraging more field trips to Asian centers, and by conducting in-service workshops for teachers.

8. *Do you believe that Asian languages should be taught in the schools?* All but one respondent answered yes. This was a 96 percent affirmative

response. The respondents believe that knowing a language will help promote international relations and international trade. Further statements include: The rapid economic growth of East Asia makes it likely to be one of the most dynamic areas of the world in the next decade. With one-fourth of the world's population speaking Chinese, knowledge of that language will prove beneficial in one's career. The inclusion of Asian language instruction in American schools, where all language teaching is presently deficient, will be symbolic of the need to get to know Asian peoples. It was also pointed out that Asians have a greater facility with the English language compared to the few Americans who know how to speak Asian tongues.

communication — Asians better with English language gives them an "edge"

SUMMARY

The results of the survey indicate that the perception of Asian Americans in America in the 1980s is generally more favorable than in earlier periods.[1] The general perception of Asian Americans, based on our survey, is that they are "industrious," "intelligent," and "inscrutable." The perception of Asians as inscrutable is probably due to the fictional character of Dr. Fu Manchu, a Chinese figure created by author Sax Rohmer that became the basis for several films in the 1930s. Asian Americans themselves regard the perception that they are "passive" and "unassertive" as the most serious. They believe that it is a misperception and must be overcome.

Recommended measures to overcome these misperceptions center around the teaching of more Asian and Asian American subjects in the schools, including the teaching of Asian languages. The survey also indicates that there are differences in patterns of communication among different Asian American groups, such as between Chinese Americans and Japanese Americans.

We cannot and should not expect Asian Americans to behave exactly like mainstream Anglo Americans. There will always be differences, but we must prevent these differences from becoming stereotypes. For example, Asian American have been characterized as industrious and intelligent. Obviously, not all Asians in this country are intelligent and industrious. Asian Americans have also been perceived as inscrutable, passive, and unassertive. Again, there are many Asians who are very articulate, assertive, and aggressive.

It is important to recognize these differences in behavior patterns as differences and not to overgeneralize or overemphasize them. Each

Asian American group has its own customs and habits, and with them there may be certain habits of thought and patterns of behavior unique to themselves. It is up to us, the general American public, to try to learn as much as we can about the cultural patterns of these new immigrant Asian groups. At the same time, Asian Americans themselves are also trying to understand and integrate into the mainstream American tradition.

To better understand the various Asian ethnic groups, Part II of this book is intended to help introduce Asian subjects and activities into the classrooms at various grade levels in the schools.

NOTES

1. Harold Isaac, *Images of Asia: American Views of China and India* (New York: Harper Torchbooks, Harper & Row, 1958), 66–88; and Cheng-Tsu Wu, ed., *"Chink!"-A Documentary History of Anti-Chinese Prejudice in America: The Ethnic Prejudice in America Series* (New York: Meridan Book/World Publishing, 1972), 108–9, 136–44.

Part II

Classroom Activities

Arts, Crafts, and Games

Understanding Cultural Diversity

Arts, Crafts, Games and Activities

Penny W. Sing

Even though Asian Americans have been a part of the fabric of American society for several generations, they are again becoming the subject of much interest and scrutiny by mainstream society. As is not uncommon in the history of minorities in America, negative stereotypes and images, along with lack of information, prove to be a barrier to true understanding of identity and cultural heritage. Part II presents student activities designed to provide information about and promote understanding of Asia and Asian Americans.

We begin with some games and arts and crafts that Asian children enjoy. These activities will stimulate an interest in and promote an understanding of Asians and various Asian American groups. The use of pictures, audio visual aids, group discussion, and role playing will greatly enhance the depth of study. Facets of these arts, crafts, games, and activities can be incorporated into the curriculum.

This part of the activities section contains 16 activities or projects chosen primarily for grade school children as icebreakers to get all the children directly involved with games and arts and crafts of Asian countries. At the same time, the students will learn about the customs and habits of Asian children. The next activities section describes 16 activities geared to junior high school, high school, and college students. These activities teach through interaction, discussion, and reading about

Asian peoples and Asian Americans, their customs and habits, their issues and concerns.

1 Calligraphy

Level: Primary through adult.

Background: In most parts of East Asia (China, Japan, and Korea), calligraphy has always been considered an art, and a person with a good calligraphic hand is highly respected. Calligraphy is like painting, but the strokes must be done in a decisive manner with no retouching. To become a good calligrapher requires years of study and concentrated practice.

Objectives: The student will

1. Learn how to hold and use a Chinese calligraphic brush;
2. Learn the basics of the Chinese number system and the writing of some simple Chinese characters; and
3. Learn about the implements of a Chinese scholar's studio—inkstone, paper, brush, and ink.

Materials: The traditional implements of the calligrapher are a brush, stand, inkstick, inkstone, and paper. To make the ink, a small amount of the inkstick is rubbed on the stone with water. The writing brush is held upright between the middle and index fingers and the thumb while the arm and wrist, flat on the table, remain motionless. Only the fingers and hand move. Nowadays, however, the ink comes ready-ground, and instead of the traditional wolf-hair brushes, soft, felt-tipped brushmarkers are available that can be substituted.

Procedure: Chinese characters, which are pictographs and ideographs, are comprised of strokes that are written in a particular order. The general rule of making the strokes of a character is from left to right and from top to bottom. When a horizontal stroke and another stroke intersect, the horizontal one usually comes first.

Traditional Chinese writing in books and scrolls was written in columns from top to bottom and across the page from right to left. But on mainland China today, the practice is to write horizontally across the page from left to right in the same manner as Westerners.

1. Since Chinese numbers are the easiest characters to write, in this first exercise, we will learn to write the numbers from one to ten. A worksheet can be made to help students learn. Use an ordinary pen or a flexible felt tip pen. Follow the direction of the arrows in executing the strokes. Use the remaining empty squares to practice the strokes, position, and proportion.

2. The number 11 is written like this 十一
   Write the number: 12   16
                      13   17
                      14   18
                      15   19
3. Twenty is written like this 二十
   Write the following: 30   70
                         40   80
                         50   90
                         60   100
4. Twenty-one is written like this 二十一
   Try writing these numbers in Chinese
   42   55   98
   74   86   67

Some Chinese shops sell special practice books with characters outlined in red ink. Brush pens, ready-ground ink, and individual ink-wells can also be purchased. If practice books are available in your community, you can remove the pages and cut them in half (the pages are double-sided). Each student is given a page, along with a brush pen and inked inkwell. The students copy the written characters.

Answers

2   十二   十六
     十三   十七
     十四   十八
     十五   十九

3   三十   七十
     四十   八十
     五十   九十
     六十   一百

4   四十二   五十五   九十八
     七十四   八十六   六十七

2 Carp Kite

Level: Upper primary and intermediate.

Background: One of the most exciting festivals in Japan used to be the celebration of Boy's Day on May 5. Brightly colored carp kites hung from tall bamboo poles in front of houses where boys lived. Each son had a banner flying in his honor. The carp was selected because it is a strong and brave fish able to leap up waterfalls. Parents hoped that these same qualities of aspiration, daring, and success would be found in their sons.

Today this festival includes girls and is known as Children's Day. The paper carp is still flown for the sons, but the real purpose of the holiday is to instill in all children the importance of being good citizens, courageous, and strong.

Objectives: The student will:

1. Learn about the celebration of a Children's holiday in Japan, much like Mother's or Father's Day here in the United States;
2. Develop skills in the construction of a carp kite, using traditional materials and techniques.

Materials:

> Large sheet of paper
> Marking pens, pencil
> White glue
> Thin wire
> Buttonhole thread or string

Directions for a paper carp kite:

1. Sketch design on paper with pencil and color in with marking pens. Cut out.
2. Fold paper in half, design on the outside. Glue edges together, except for the mouth and tail.
3. Form a circle with the wire, the same circumference as the mouth. Apply glue to inside edge of mouth, put wire in place and fold edge 1/2-inch over wire.

4. Make a harness with the thread or string and attach to a pole or hang it from the ceiling in your classroom.

Directions for a cloth carp kite:

1. The carp kite can also be made from cloth. Be sure to add a seam allowance on lengthwise edges.
2. Fold the design to the inside and stitch by hand or machine along lengthwise edges. Do not stitch the mouth or tail openings.
3. Turn fish right side out.
4. Attach wire circle to inside of mouth.
5. Turn fabric over the wire to form a 1/2-inch hem.
6. Sew hem by hand.

3 Chinese Name Chop or Seal (The Chinese equivalent of your signature)

Level: Upper primary and intermediate.

Background: The name chop or seal was and still is an important part of the ritual of signing documents and concluding important transactions. The chops are used as personal seals on letters, documents, and artwork. They are inked with a red paste, appearing as red letters on white or white letters on red when pressed onto documents and papers that require the owner's signature.

Chinese name chops are usually carved from special kinds of stone, ivory, or jade. Both ends of the chop are beautiful; the printing end holds characters, which are the owner's name. The top of the chop often has a delicately carved animal.

Traditionally, the Chinese signature consists of the family name first, then one or two characters of the given name. In some families all the children of the same generation, brothers, sisters, and cousins, have the same middle character. This simplifies genealogical study.

Objectives: The student will

1. Learn about the importance of a seal in Chinese and Japanese society;
2. Learn about the mechanics of carving a seal.

Materials:

Art gum eraser
Pencil
Mirror
Paper
Red poster paint and brush or red ink pad
Sharp knife or razor blade

Directions:

1. Write or print your name or initials or make a simple design on paper. Make a border around the four sides. If you are making letters, draw them in reverse. Use the mirror to help.

2. Hold the art gum eraser vertically on the table. Using the pencil, transfer the design onto the end of the eraser.
3. With the sharp knife, cut into the eraser about 1/8-inch and remove the area behind the letter or design.
4. Apply red poster paint with the brush to the surface of the chop or stamp it on an ink pad. Press firmly onto paper.
5. You can repeat the process on the other side of the eraser. You may wish to experiment and cut out the letter or design this time to create another style.

4   Chinese New Year Parade

Level: Intermediate and high school

Background: An exciting event for an entire class or several classes is the performance of a Chinese New Year Parade. In China, Hong Kong, Taiwan, and large Chinatowns across North America, a large parade is held in celebration of the Chinese New Year. The purpose is to ensure good luck and good fortune and to drive away bad luck for the future.

A common sight in these celebrations is the lion following his "teaser," a happy Buddhist monk who loves animals. The lion dances to the noise of drums and firecrackers to drive out evil spirits. When the parade reaches the shops, the lion receives a red envelope of lucky money for his services. Sometimes the shopkeepers make the lion work hard by placing the red envelope inside a head of cabbage and dangling it from a second-story window. The lion will prance around, jump onto another man's shoulders, grab the cabbage in its mouth, and pretend to eat it before getting the money.

The dragon is another popular figure in parades. Some large Chinese communities in North America use it for special celebrations. The dragon's body is very large and long. It is held up on sticks and is swung rhythmically back and forth by 25 men or more, depending upon its size.

Objectives: The student will learn about one of the most important festivals in East Asia and how to put on a celebration for the occasion.

Implementation: Directions for making your own lion or dragon can be found in *Chinese Cultural Activities, vol. I,* an Arts, Inc. publication (New York, 1977). You may be able to rent or borrow these from local organizations in your community.

A great deal of noise is required for accompaniment in the parade. You will need someone playing a big drum and several children with gongs and cymbals so that the lion dance rhythms can be made. For additional noise, rhythm sticks, small drums, pebbles in cans, and tambourines can be used.

Since firecrackers are forbidden in schools, simulated strings of giant ones can be made by rolling red tissue paper around an empty toilet paper roll. Twist the ends and put them towards the inside. Attach the "firecracker" to a dowel with string. Some children could carry and wave these in the parade. Other children could carry bright-colored lanterns, also attached to dowels with string. Follow the directions from the Origami activity on page 51 for making the lantern, but use the larger piece of colored paper, at least 16 inches square. This could be decorated by adding a tissue paper cut-out of the character "spring," since the celebration of the New Year also denotes the coming of spring. Fold the tissue paper in half and trace the following outline. Cut and open up. Glue to lantern front with rubber cement.

Some children can wear a fancy Chinese jacket, holding a face mask, a fan, or a small toy paper dragon. Others can pose as a martial arts troupe, wearing T-shirts, wide sashes, and black or colored warm up pants, gathered at the ankles.

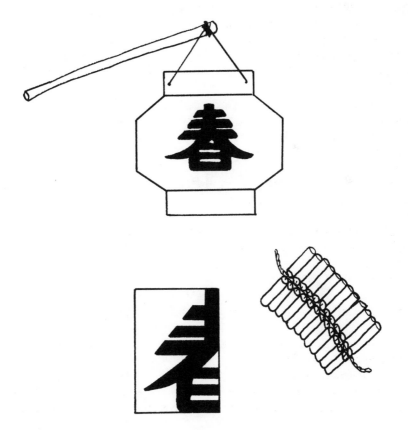

The parade should march around the auditorium, then go up to the stage. Each group should pause and perform its special skill for a minute as it crosses the stage. The musicians should sit at the side of the stage, playing loud rhythms as the others pass by.

This activity is a fun way to get many people involved. However, because of the excitement and noise generated, it is best to plan the parade as the last event of the school day.

5 Jianzi, Kicking the Chinese Shuttlecock

Level: Primary through adult.

Background: A favorite game of Chinese children for thousands of years was kicking a shuttlecock known as the *jianzi* (Chinese), *jae gee* (Korean). Perhaps it was invented to help them stay warm during the cold winters in northern China.

    The traditional shuttlecock was made from an old Chinese coin with a hole in the middle. Goose quills were poked into the hole and the coin was wrapped in soft leather. The object of the game was to keep the shuttlecock in the air for as long as possible, always catching it on the side (either the inside or outside, depending on the degree of the kicker's proficiency) of the foot. It is best to wear the traditional cotton-padded shoes, customary in north China. However a pair of sneakers would do fine. A good player could send the shuttlecock high into the air vertically and keep it going for hundreds of strokes. Shuttlecock kicking provides good exercise while playing. Thus it helped the children keep warm and fit while having fun.

Objectives: The student will learn about this popular sport and exercise in East Asia and how to make a Chinese-style shuttlecock.

Materials: There are two ways to make the *jianzi*.

1. With chicken feathers:
   1-inch washer or Chinese coin or several 1-inch cardboard disks
   2 pieces   5/8-inch vinyl disks
   1 straight plastic bead
   3 to 6 chicken feathers
   white glue
   buttonhole thread or dental floss
   needle
2. With rug yarn:
   1-inch washer or Chinese coin with hole in the center
   rug yarn cut in pieces 8 to 10 inches long

Directions: With chicken feathers:

1. Cut a small hole in the center of one vinyl disk the same diameter as the bead.
2. Place coin, washer, or cardboard disks between the two vinyl disks.
3. Thread needle with thread or floss. Knot end, then whip stitch around the two vinyl disks. Secure end.
4. Glue feathers into the bead, then glue bead through the hole in the top disk. Let dry thoroughly before using.

Directions: With yarn:

1. Fold each piece of yarn in half.
2. Pass the folded end of the yarn through the hole in the washer.
3. Wrap the cut ends around the washer and pass them through the folded end. Pull tightly.
4. Repeat until the disk is covered with yarn.

To Play: Setting up for a kick with the hand is permitted. Kick the shuttlecock with the inner side and the sole of your foot, both forward and backward. Any number may play, standing in a rough circle; players who miss are out. You may also play the game as individuals; the player who keeps the *jianzi* up the longest is the winner.

6   Daruma Doll

Level: Primary through intermediate.

Background: The *daruma* is one of Japan's most popular folk toys. It is a good luck charm often purchased during the beginning of the New Year with hopes it will bring good fortune. The word is derived from Bodhidharma, the Indian Buddhist priest who brought Buddhism to China. Legends say that Bodhidharma sat in silent meditation for nine years. This inactivity caused the loss of movement in his arms and legs.

Thus, *darumas* are made with no arms or legs. They have weighted, rounded bottoms so that they will return to an upright position, no matter how often they are knocked down. This symbolizes a spirit of perseverance and determination, admirable qualities for people to attain.

There are many kinds of *darumas* and the facial characteristics vary from region to region. One of the most charming traditions associated with the toy is the wishing *daruma*. It has blank eyes with no iris. One iris is painted on when you make a wish. When the wish comes true, the other iris is painted on.

Objectives: The student will learn the symbolism and use of the *daruma* in Japan.

Materials:

> Empty L'eggs or plastic egg
> Plasticene or dough
> Glue
> Newspaper strips, regular and comic sections
> Lightweight cardboard
> Poster paint: red, flesh, yellow or gold, black, white
> Lacquer or shellac
> Wheat paste
> Scotch tape

Directions:

1. Anchor plasticene with glue to the lower half of the plastic egg. Put the egg together.

2. Soak newspaper strips in wheat paste, removing excess, and apply to entire egg. Alternate regular and comic sections until five layers have been applied over the egg. Let dry.
3. To frame the facial features, roll a piece of newspaper 7 1/2 inches X 12 inches to about pencil size. Tape onto the doll to make a ridged outline of the face. Cut tape in place.
4. Cover entire face area, ridge and nose, with three layers of newspaper strips which have been dipped in the wheat paste mixture. Let dry.
5. Paint the face with flesh-colored paint and the rest of the doll with red poster paint.
6. Paint facial features. For a high gloss finish, apply a coat of lacquer or shellac.

7   Jan Ken Po (Scissors, Stone, Cloth)

Level: Primary.

Background: This game, well known to children in many lands, originated in Japan. The children often use it for choosing who will take the first turn in a game or activity or for settling a tie.

Objectives: The students will learn about one of the simplest and most popular children's games in East Asia.

Directions: Hand positions

> Jan (scissors): middle and index fingers extended.
> Ken (stone): clenched fist.
> Po (cloth): hand held open, fingers outstretched.

The game is played in pairs. Each player chants the words, "jan, ken, po," as he or she shakes one fist up and down. After "po" has been said, he or she must form one of the three positions. The winner is determined as follows:

> Scissors beats cloth (by cutting).
> Cloth beats stone (by wrapping it up).
> Stone beats scissors (by blunting them).

If both players make the same position, they repeat the process until one wins.

8   Haiku Poetry

Level: Primary through adult.

Background: *Haiku* is a Japanese nonrhyming poem that suggests a mood or picture, often a season of the year. It contains 17 syllables and usually three lines:

> First line: the setting of the poem (five syllables).
> Second line: the action (seven syllables).
> Third line: the conclusion or feeling (five syllables).

Example:

> A windy spring day
> The kites soar above the clouds.
> I want to fly too.

Objectives: The student will learn how to write a short, lyrical poem expressing personal feelings.

Application: After a class outing, especially a nature trip, suggest that students write a modified haiku—a one or two line descriptive phrase about something that impressed or delighted them. For example, "Yellow leaves swirled like a top in the breeze." This could then be expanded into the regular haiku format.

9 Origami

Level: Primary through adult.

Background: *Origami* is the art of paper folding (*ori* means to fold, and *gami* is paper). Although *origami* originated centuries ago in China, it was the Japanese who popularized the craft by incorporating it into their school curriculum. All children learn how, without cutting or pasting, to create animals, flowers, dolls, and many other objects.

Today, *origami* is practiced mainly for pleasure; since the end of World War II, it has become an increasingly popular art form for adults. The Friends of the Origami Center of America in New York City grew in several years to over 1,000 members. Your library contains many good books on *origami*. Just as an introduction, instructions are given here on how to fold a lantern.

Objectives: The student will learn the art of paper folding and to fold a paper lantern.

Materials: Pre-cut *origami* paper, 8 or 10 inches square. You can experiment with different weights of paper.

Directions:

1. Fold paper in half. Unfold.
2. Fold both sides to the center. This is a cupboard door base.
3. Fold up the bottom corners (valley fold) to meet in the center.
4. Fold the pointed end to the back (mountain fold).
5. Valley fold the bottom corners to meet in the center of the front again.
6. Turn the paper over and flatten the split diamond shape at the bottom to form the rim.
7. Turn the paper over. Repeat the process from step three for the other end. This completes the lantern.

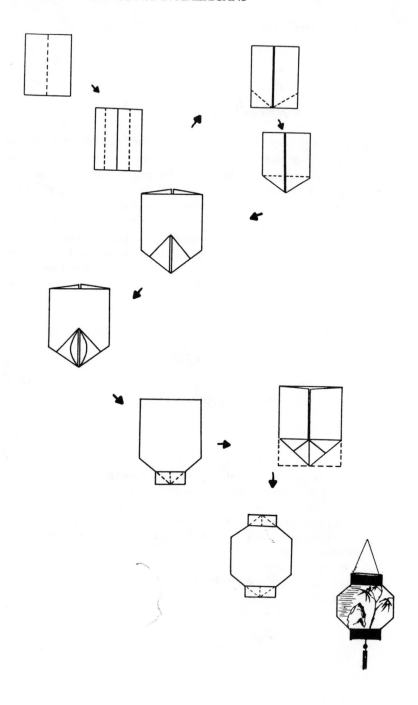

10 Paper Cutting

Level: Primary through adult.

Background: Paper cuts of colored paper began to appear during the Tang Dynasty (618 to 906 A.D.). The paper cuts were once used as guides to make wood blocks for printing and as stencils on lacquerware and pottery. When tacked onto cloth, they served as guides for embroiderer's designs. Paper cuts were often used as decorations on paper-covered windows and for gifts, especially during holidays.

Today, paper cutting has developed into a fold art. There are several ways to cut a design. Fold a sheet of paper in half or quarters, cutting a symmetrical design. Whole scenes or objects can be cut in a freehand style by drawing a rough sketch on the back of the paper and then cutting it without folding.

Objectives: The student will develop skills in the art of paper cutting.

Two Chinese characters, one meaning longevity (the Chinese character is pronounced *show*), the other meaning happiness (pronounced *shi* as in *shin*) will be cut out.

Materials:

> Paper: square tissue or colored paper such as origami-type construction
>   paper
> Scissors
> Rubber cement

Directions: *Happiness*—Fold tissue or colored paper into quarters and place cut out pattern on the folded edge. Cut and open up design.

Longevity—Attach tissue paper cut to colored construction paper with rubber cement. The residue can be rolled away with your fingers. Use it as a greeting card, wall decoration, or note paper.

Happiness—

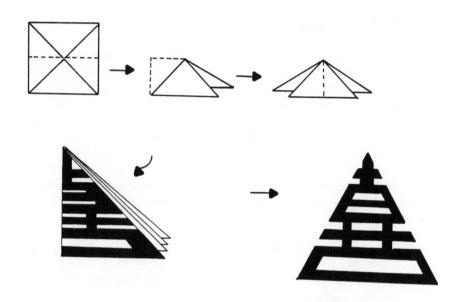

Longevity—

11   Tangram Puzzle

Level: Primary through adult.

Background: Chinese folklore tells us that tangrams were accidentally invented by a nobleman who dropped a square ceramic tile, which broke into seven pieces. When he tried to reassemble the pieces, he discovered over 1,000 interesting patterns and designs.

Today, tangrams are regarded as a child's game. When they were brought to the United States and Europe in the 1800s, they fascinated well-known people like Napoleon, Lewis Carroll, and Edgar Allan Poe. They would spend hours forming pictures of animals, walking figures, boats, geometric shapes, and silhouettes. The game can be made more decorative by making the pieces different colors or by combining several sets.

Objectives: The student will learn how to construct a tangram puzzle and to piece the geometric shapes into different objects.

Materials:

> Cardboard
> Scissors

Directions: Reproduce the pattern below. Cut out the 7 shapes with scissors.

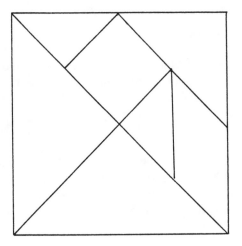

Try to make these designs:

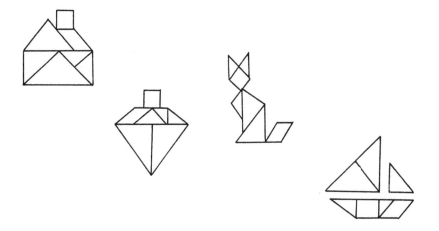

What other patterns or designs can you make? Can you remake the tile into its original square shape?

12 Khokad: Indian-Style Tag

Level: Primary.

Background: This game of tag is usually played on a festive occasion, such as on the birthday celebration of Mahatma Gandhi on October 2 when there is a Sound-and-Light show. But it can be done any time to give the students the experience of playing this game.

Objectives: The students will learn this Indian form of tag and the occasion on which it is usually played.

Procedure: The game can be played with 15 to 20 students. They are divided evenly into sitters and standers. The sitters will squat in a row in a straight line about three feet apart but facing opposite directions. The standers will stand opposite every other sitter, one in front and one in back.

The captain of the sitters begins the game by circling the group several times. Then he or she shouts, "Standers beware!" and tries to tag the standers. Any player tagged is out of the game. The standers can cross the row of sitters to avoid being tagged, but the captain cannot cross over and can only circle around in one direction. However, the captain can touch the head of one of the sitters on the line who can continue the chase; the captain takes the place of that sitter. The captain can only circle the group in one direction; he or she cannot reverse the direction.

After all the standers are tagged, the roles are changed and the game continues. In the illustration the filled circles are the standers, and the blank circles are the sitters. The arrows on the sitters indicate the direction that each one is facing.

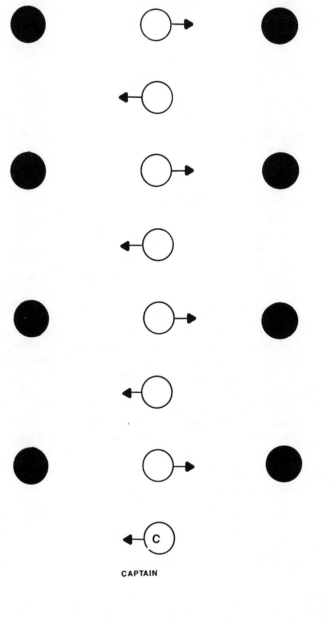

CAPTAIN

STANDERS

SITTERS

13   Alpana: Good Luck Designs

Level: Upper primary.

Background: During the *Diwali* festival, one of the most important holidays in India usually celebrated in October or November, good luck designs, called *alpana,* are made on the ground in front of one's home. The designs are either abstract or traditional folk motifs and are decorated with colored rice flour. Rice flour is used because rice symbolizes abundance and welcome. In some cities, contests are held, and the most beautiful *alpana* gets a prize.

The festival, also know as the Festival of the Lamps, is held in honor of Lakshmi, who is the goddess of wealth and bliss, the wife of the god Vishnu. Special *dipa* lamps are made to be placed in front of a home altar with a picture of Lakshmi. At night the lamps are placed on the roofs of buildings to attract the blessings of the goddess.

Objectives: The student will learn about the *Diwali* festival and the traditional method of making *alpana* designs.

Materials:

> Assorted colors of powdered poster paint
> Shallow cardboard boxes
> Sand or sterilized potting soil
> Rice flour
> Small bowls
> Aluminum foil or wax paper
> Scissors

Procedure: Line the box with foil or wax paper, spread a layer of damp sand or soil on the bottom. Make the surface smooth. Sketch a design on the surface. Mix a small amount of powdered paint with the rice flour in a small bowl. Then make a cone with a piece of paper; scotch tape it firmly. Snip off just the tip of the cone. Then pour the paint and flour mixture into the cone, but be sure to plug the hole with your finger. Now bring the cone over to your design, unplug the hole, and gently trace around the design you have made. Traditional designs are the face of Lakshmi or a lotus flower.

Other related activities: Students can also learn to make a *diwali* lamp. Take some air-drying clay and shape it into a shallow bowl with a little spout for the wick. Let the bowl harden overnight. Then fill it half full with salad oil. Put a wick in the oil and light it (be sure the open flame is not left unattended).

14 Games Children Play

Level: Primary.

Background: Many times children do not have contact with their own cultural roots. For Asian American children who have been raised primarily in the United States it can be enlightening to learn what children do in their ancestral lands. For non-Asian American children activities such as learning the games that children in other parts of the world play is an entry into global learning and multicultural education.

Objectives: Students will:

1. Learn some words in another language through the songs/games from another country.
2. Learn a poem or song in another language.

Implementation: Teachers do *not* have to be from the same ethnic group or ancestral background as the children in class to create this activity. Older students can be assigned to bring a favorite short baby rhyme or song typical of their ancestral lands. The students should be encouraged to use parents or grandparents as a resource for this project. The children will have to know the rhymes well enough to explain and teach them to the class.

Parents and grandparents can be invited to teach one song or game to the class. The teacher should write out the words in some comprehensible phonetic script so that the class can refer back to them. The songs or rhymes can be collected in a notebook for other classes. Parents and grandparents from several different cultural background should be invited so that no children feel that their ethnic group is being focused on or, on the other hand, that their background is being ignored.

15   What's in a Name

Level: Upper primary.

Background: Names are very personal identifiers and also represent an important part of ethnic history. They also reflect cultural norms and traditions that are different around the world but offer deep insights into cultural backgrounds. Children may be unaware of the significance of their names. Names are an entry into learning about the values of other cultural groups.

Objective: The student will discover what is in a name. What does it mean? How did it come about? How was it chosen or given?

Implementation: Each child or pair of children will research the meaning and origin of his or her own or a relative's first and last (family) names. The child should learn how the name is pronounced in the native language; how it is spelled; why the person was given this name; who chose the name; when it was given (how old the baby was); how the name was announced (birth announcement or ceremony); how many names in all the person was given. Each child will report this information to the class. Then the class can create a bulletin board display of their names and/or relatives and historical roots reflected in these.

Students and teachers often love to see how their name would be pronounced and/or written in another language. If some of the children come from another language background, an adult from the community could be invited to make name tags or plates for each child in the ancestral script.

16 Chopsticks Game: Pick up the beans

Level: Primary through adult.

Background: Most people in East Asian and Southeast Asian countries use chopsticks for eating instead of knives and forks. Chopsticks are used to grasp, pick up, and divide rice, noodles, vegetables, fish, meat, and just about everything (except soup). Large, long chopsticks are also used for cooking.

This activity helps participants learn to hold and use a pair of chopsticks. Chopsticks may be made of various kinds of materials, from inexpensive wood or bamboo to costly lacquer, or silver.

Materials:

1. A pair of chopsticks for each student (obtainable from any Chinese or Japanese restaurant);
2. A plate or bowl for each student; and
3. A bag of dried beans (large beans, such as lima or kidney beans).

Procedure:

1. Each student is given two bowls; one is empty, and the other contains five or ten beans.
2. Each student is also given a pair of chopsticks and directions on how to hold and use them.
3. The teacher demonstrates how to use the chopsticks and shows how the student should transfer the beans from one bowl to the other.
4. After some practice, the students may have a contest to see who is the fastest in transferring the beans from one bowl to the other. The first one who finishes wins.

Variation: Divide the class into three or four equal groups. The teacher distributes the same number of beans to the first person in each group. Each person has a bowl and a pair of chopsticks. The object of the game is to transfer the beans from your bowl to the bowl of the person next in line. The group that finishes first wins.

Directions for holding and using chopsticks:

1. Place one chopstick under base of thumb and middle finger of right or left hand (see illustration 1).
2. Add second chopstick. Hold as if you are holding a pencil (see illustration 2).
3. Hold first chopstick in original position, then move the second one up and down. Try picking up an object by manipulating the second chopstick (see illustration 3).

Note: Beginners learn how difficult it is to use chopsticks, but the advanced user learns how easy and versatile chopsticks really are. The connoisseur says that Chinese and Japanese food tastes better with chopsticks.

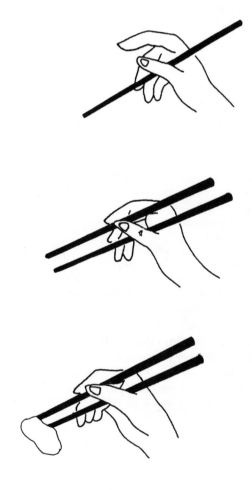

Understanding Cultural Diversity

Joyce Penfield

Whereas the first section of Part II was devoted to exploring games and cultural artifacts of Asia, this part focuses on the understanding of cultural diversity and awareness of cultural differences within the context of our multicultural society.

The following instructional activities are designed to promote positive and realistic views of Asian American history, cultural and religious history, language background, and values. The activities are either short-term or long-term projects and are intended to be used as a supplement to on-going classroom instruction in a variety of disciplines. The activities are multi-cultural in nature: their goal is to promote positive views of all ethnic backgrounds represented in a given class. The emphasis here, however, is on the ethnic background typical of different Asian Americans. The ultimate goal of the activities is to instill a sense of worth and understanding of ethnic variation—be it one's own or that of others.

The activities engage students in the examination of Asian Americans' past, present, and future. They focus on the following aspects:

1. Critical examination of negative vs. positive images and stereotypes of Asian Americans presented in literature, history, textbooks, and the media.
2. Discovery of ancestral and cultural roots reflected in games, how children lived, names and naming, geography, etc.

3. Examination of culture through analyzing value orientation, style of living, cross-generational changes, and family roles.
4. Exploration of future goals related to career goals and life-styles.

1 Asian Americans in Literature

Level: Secondary

Background: Our images of others are formed through various means—the media, literature, and interpersonal contact. Literature written by outsiders or those distanced from a particular ethnic group may reflect negative stereotypical views of that group. If students do not read critically, they may take these "images" as real and operate with false assumptions about others. An educated reader should be aware of the context of views presented by authors in order to evaluate them critically.

Objectives:

1. Identify stereotypes in literature.
2. Identify themes of Asian American experiences as expressed in literature.

Materials: Select a short story or novel portraying a particular Asian group—Chinese, Japanese, Korean, Filipino, Vietnamese, etc.—that was written 20 or 30 years ago and reflects a certain bias. For a stereotypical portrayal of the Chinese, see James Clavell's *Tai-pan* (New York: Dell, 1978).

Select another short story or novel portraying Asians or Asian Americans written more recently. Readings from Hsu and Palubinskas, *Asian-American Authors,* and Chin, et al., *Aiiieeeee!* would be an excellent source for short stories and autobiographical pieces. See Part IV. Annotated Bibliography, General Works on Asia and Asian Americans, page 125.

Provide the students with a literature question guide that includes the following:

1. What assumptions are made about the nature and role of this ethnic group in this piece of literature?
2. What themes emerge regarding the dilemma of this ethnic group?
3. How are members of this ethnic group portrayed (as devils, angels, animals, sly, intelligent, etc.)? Describe them. How are males presented differently from females?

4. How do these characters speak? What language or what type of English do they use?
5. Who wrote the piece of literature and in what historical setting or period was it written? How did this affect the writer?

Implementation: All students should read both short stories and novels. Divide the students into small groups of three or four and have each group discuss the answers to the questions. Each group should compare and contrast the two pieces of literature. Have each group report back to the entire class on what it discovered. Divide the blackboard into two parts and make a list of the authors' perceptions portrayed in each piece of literature. Perhaps stereotypical depictions will be immediately obvious. In case of doubt consult an expert. Also see the survey results in part one of this volume.

2 Careers

Level: Secondary.

Background: Many students only consider a limited number of career options because they have never seen certain ethnic persons filling nontraditional occupational roles. It is, therefore, important to expose ethnic groups to nonstereotypical roles and to those people in the community from their ethnic backgrounds who have been successful in nontraditional work/career roles.

Objective: The students will share their attitudes on ethnic stereotyping related to the professions.

Implementation: Have class members bring in pictures of workers from a particular ethnic group found in magazines, newspapers, etc., or have students think of jobs associated with particular ethnic groups and list as many as possible. The teacher writes the students' suggestions on the board. Ask various class members what their parents do professionally and which ethnic group they belong to. Then elicit examples of kinds of work done by members of this ethnic group. Discuss why we associate these occupations with this particular ethnic group. Discuss what qualities influence success on the job (interest, abilities, performance, ethnic background).

Follow up: Invite parents to come in and talk about their professions: what they do; how they got into particular fields; what preparation was needed; what future possibilities they have; what they like and dislike about their professions.

3 The Media's Portrayal

Level: Secondary.

Background: The characteristics of people portrayed by the media often reflect ethnic stereotypes. Even certain eras in the history of an ethnic group may be stereotyped. One prominent example is *Shogun*. Students need to learn to think critically and become aware of the stereotypical notions that television assumes and reproduces.

Objectives:

1. Identify stereotypical characteristics portrayed by the media or movies;
2. Compare media perceptions with reality;
3. Identify how media portrayals distort and magnify historical reality.

Materials:

1. TV program (provide students with channel, time, and day).
2. A popular movie, e.g. *Return of the Dragon*, videotaped or seen before class.

Implementation: Have students watch an assigned show in groups if possible, either in their homes or in class. For each show note down the following for each character:

> Name of character:
> Ethnic group/country:
> Language:
> Profession/Job:
> Clothes and physical appearance:
> Actions:
> Your reaction to this character (what you liked or disliked about the character):

Have each group compare and compile notes. Each group should write one description of this ethnic group as portrayed by the program. This description may be a written report, pictures, a skit, or bulletin board display. Encourage creativity. Each group will then discuss what it found. Discuss how each television show or movie portrayed stereotypes of an ethnic group. Contrast with reality.

4   My Image of . . .

Level: Intermediate.

Background: Everyone operates with images of certain places and people. Television and other media encourage some very distorted images of different cultures. Students need to become aware of their images and how those images do not always reflect the sum total of variation within any given culture, or how the views of a given culture are distorted and exaggerated.

Objectives:

1. Generate images of an Asian American group, such as Japanese, Chinese, Korean, or Vietnamese.
2. Work on undoing negative or oversimplified images (to replace them with more accurate ones).
3. The same activity can be applied to people who live in Asian countries such as China, Japan, Korea, etc.

Activity: Ask students to write down phrases describing what they associate with the Chinese (some students could do Japanese, others Koreans, others Vietnamese, etc.). Second, students should draw quick pictures of their visual images.

Teachers will engage class in a discussion of what the words and pictures say about the students' images of these people. Students will discuss where their images came from. Then the teacher will assign a research project to the class so that they can learn accurate information about the Chinese, Japanese, Koreans, etc. Some project questions could include:

1. How do the Chinese (Japanese, Koreans, Vietnamese) differ from other peoples?
2. What kinds of leisurely and occupational activities do they participate in?
3. What do their houses and clothes look like?
4. What is their natural environment like?
5. What's important to the Chinese (Japanese, Koreans, Vietnamese)?

5 Our Stereotypes

Level: Secondary.

Background: Stereotypes are a means of categorizing others based on incomplete perceptions. These perceptions can be harmful if they create barriers to openness in discovering the range of variation inherent in any cultural or ethnic group.

Objectives:

1. Identify the qualities that students view as typical of another ethnic group;
2. Identify the qualities that they view as most valued, unvalued, and least valued in their own culture.

Implementation: Have students rate their own and another ethnic group using the following list of qualities. Rate an ethnic group, then rate your own ethnic group, then yourself as an individual, and an individual of another ethnic group. Discuss your rating with other members of the class. A check mark in position (1) means "most valued," position (3) means "unvalued" or neutral, and a check in position (5) means "least valued."

	1	2	3	4	5
Aggressiveness	——	——	——	——	——
Independence	——	——	——	——	——
Privacy	——	——	——	——	——
Education	——	——	——	——	——
Submissiveness	——	——	——	——	——
Excitability	——	——	——	——	——
Competitiveness	——	——	——	——	——
Rationality	——	——	——	——	——
Family-oriented	——	——	——	——	——
Adventurousness	——	——	——	——	——
Leadership	——	——	——	——	——
Inner peace	——	——	——	——	——
True friendship	——	——	——	——	——

Harmony   ___   ___   ___   ___   ___
Money   ___   ___   ___   ___   ___

Discuss how these qualities can be an advantage to you and how they can work against you.

6 Famous Asian Americans

Level: Intermediate and secondary.

Background: Often inaccurate views of Asian Americans are presented in U.S. history textbooks or there is no mention of the participation of Asian Americans in the development of the United States. Teachers must provide opportunities for students to learn about the real struggles of minority groups in the history of America. The truth about how these minorities were treated at different points in history should also be revealed.

Objectives: Students will learn about

1. The contribution of Asian Americans to the development of the United States as a nation;
2. Some specific Asian American folk heroes.

Materials: Students will consult the bibliographic section of this book for resources.

Implementation: Pairs of students will engage in historical research about figures from American history. Have students read and discuss autobiographical information on the roles of Asian Americans in U.S. history. Let each pair select an individual to study. Provide the resources and time. Be careful to select individuals from as many different Asian American cultural groups as possible (Vietnamese, People's Republic of China, Taiwan, Japan, Korea, Philippines, India, Pakistan, etc.). Also try to select an equal number of women and men.

Each pair of students will complete a project that will collectively form a historical notebook on famous Asian Americans as well as a bulletin board display on "Famous Asian Americans in Our Country." Each pair will present their data in any of the following creative ways: pictures, oral reports, skits, paintings, music and dance, or puppets about their historical character.

7 "This Is Your Life"—Oral History

Level: Intermediate and secondary.

Background: Community members are a seldom tapped but rich resource for learning. First- and second-generation children of immigrants and refugees can develop a more positive image of themselves by uncovering details about their roots/ancestry. Unless the teacher specifically assigns such an activity, children may never learn about their own ancestral history.

Objectives: Students will:

1. Expand their knowledge of their own and others' cultural backgrounds;
2. Learn to research oral history.

Implementation: The student should find a first-generation immigrant who will talk about his or her experiences. He or she could be a friend or relative. The following is a list of sample questions that the student may ask the informant.

1. Respondent's name, age, and sex
2. Relationship to student
3. Ethnic group
4. Occupation (now and former)
5. Did you live most of your life on a farm or in the city?
6. Where did you live mostly as a child?
7. How old were you when you first came to this country?
8. What were some of your first impressions as an immigrant?
9. Did it take you long to adjust to American life?
10. Were there language barriers?
11. Do you feel comfortable living in America now?

8 Family Roles

Level: Secondary.

Background: Students can understand themselves and their families better if they can identify factors that affect how the family limits or increases the options for changing family living patterns. Often self-concepts and feelings about one's ethnic background are influenced significantly by factors that in turn determine the family's lifestyle.

Objectives: Students will become aware of at least ten family roles and identify five roles they play in their own family structures. They will identify variations in roles from family to family according to traditional ethnic background and contemporary American culture.

Implementation: Each student will draw a wagon-wheel design with five spokes and put his or her name in the center; each spoke will represent the different roles he or she plays in the family such as: taking care of younger siblings, cooking for the family, working in the family business, or participating in cultural and religious celebrations. The student will write one role per spoke. On another paper each student will also list the people he or she interacts with in each role and what is expected of them. Students will compare their wheels and discuss their role differences.

The following discussion questions might be used:

1. Are your roles in the family influenced by your ethnic background? How?
2. Are there different behaviors expected or allowed for girls and boys in your family? What are the differences?
3. Do you think the roles you play now will be those you will expect your children to play? Why? Why not?
4. What kind of roles do your grandparents play in your family? Your uncles? Your cousins?

9 Myths in History Class

Level: Secondary.

Background: Often a history class or a social studies textbook will present an institutionalized myth such as the "melting pot" theory of acculturation. These myths sometimes perpetuate an idealized image of our country as a land of liberty and freedom, glossing over such harsh realities as slavery before the pre-Civil War and anti-Asian legislation in the West (see Appendix B). Students should know the truth about their own heritage and the contribution of other cultural groups that make up American society.

Objective: Students will examine U.S. history for contributions of Asian Americans.

Implementation: The teacher will assign topics for investigation. Consult the bibliography in this book for resources. Possible topics for research could be contributions of Asian Americans in:

- agriculture,
- architecture,
- chemistry,
- physics,
- railroad building,
- medicine,
- culture and the arts,
- business and industry,
- literature.

10 Film as Catalyst

Level: Secondary.

Background: As the old Chinese saying goes "a picture is worth a thousand words." A film, then, is worth at least a book. A film, because of its visual impact, can make a deep impression on its viewers. The use of a good film can save many hours of reading and explanation.

Objectives: Students will:

1. Learn to transcend their own cultural bonds, values, and perceptions;
2. Examine their own individual values and attitudes.

Materials: A documentary, travelogue, or video anthropology film. (See resources suggested below.) Possible films include: *But What If the Dream Comes True* (about suburban American lifestyles); *Hunger in America* (CBS documentary); *The Inheritance* (mass migrations to America from Europe, the sweat shops, and how various ethnic groups lived). Jean Marie Ackerman's *Films of a Changing World: A Critical International Guide* and Bernice Chu's *The Asian American Media Reference Guide* would be useful here. See Richard Lacey, Seeing with Feeling: Film in the Classroom (Philadelphia: W.B. Saunders, 1972).

Implementation: The teacher should introduce the film and clearly state its purpose—not summarize the film or give its meaning. Immediately after the film is viewed, the discussion leader will steer the discussion into "feeling" and "affective" responses to the film to encourage the sharing of perceptions and feelings rather than intellectual comments. The leader should ask each student to mention a particular image or sound from the film that immediately comes to his or her mind. From this point a discussion can be led. Some topics that might create lively discussion are:

1. breakdown of the family in the United States,
2. teenage delinquency,
3. plight of the minorities, and
4. materialism.

11 Cross-Generational Change

Level: Intermediate and secondary.

Background: Part of our present self is composed of or built on our perception of our personal past.

Objective: Students will:

1. Become aware of differences in life goals across three generations in different ethnic groups;
2. Learn some oral history from their relatives and friends.

Resources: Older members of ethnic groups

Implementation: Students should interview three people, representing three different generations but from the same ethnic group, e.g. a grandmother, father, and older brother or cousin. Ask the following questions:

1. What did he or she want to be (professionally) when he or she was a child?
2. What was life like as a child?
3. What profession did he or she eventually pursue and why?

Students make a comparison of the differences between generations and report their discoveries to the class. The class discussion should center on *change*—primarily cultural and linguistic change—in order to make some inferences as to why there were or were not differences in the opportunities and aspirations of the different generations.

12 Geographic Ethnocentrism

Level: Intermediate and secondary.

Background: Most people perceive their country or continent to be the center of the world. They lose sight of their country's relation to the rest of the world and may have a distorted perception of the country's geographic position or population density.

Content: Geography, social studies.

Objectives:

1. To become more aware of how perceptions compare with reality.
2. To become aware of how each person's perceptions are centered from self and the differences that can exist around the world consequently.

Materials: Pencils and large pieces of paper; two maps of the world.

Implementation: Have each student draw a map of the world. Do not explain why or how detailed. Simply give everyone five minutes to put as much information as possible on his or her map. Students are not to help one another or look at each other's work at this time. Then, have students compare their maps and discuss how they differ. Bring out a map of the world or several different ones, and have the students discuss how they differ. Have the students compare how their versions differ from the accurate maps. What countries or continents are the largest and at the center in their maps? What countries or continents are the largest and at the center of an accurate map?

The teacher's discussion should include the following questions:

1. Why did this happen?
2. What does this mean about how each of us thinks of the world?
3. How would the students draw the map if they did it again? Why?

13 Tour Guide

Level: Secondary.

Background: Students can learn and recall more about the geographic location of people around the world by being actively involved in researching this information.

Objective: Students will discover more about geography as it relates to a specific part of the world.

Implementation: Students are to imagine that they are travel consultants and must plan a trip for a customer to a particular part of the world. (Students could be restricted to only Asia or another part of the world for this assignment.) Students should work in groups of four or five. Each group is to select a particular country and to research everything about the location. Then they should draw up an itinerary and schedule for their customer in the form of a travel package, which will later be presented to the customer. The package should include photos, visuals, maps, travel information, money exchange rates, foreign language information, and customs to be observed. Each group will share this information with the entire class.

14 Self Awareness

Level: Teachers.

Background: We all have prejudices and biases even though we may not be aware of them. It is most important that a teacher of ethnic studies or courses having to do with interracial or intercultural relations be aware of his or her own biases and try to correct them. Otherwise all his or her good intentions may be wasted.

Objective: The main objective of this exercise is to make the teacher more aware of biases in order to better understand others.

Implementation: Begin very simply by writing a brief autobiography—one or two handwritten pages. Write about yourself, where you were born, where you were raised, your job, your education, your interests, your family, your hobbies, interesting experiences, your travels, turning points in your life, and contacts with people of other cultures.

From writing about yourself, you will become more conscious of your own background, where you come from, and what attitudes you inherited from your family or social group. You should also become more aware of your present situation, your attitudes toward current events, problems, and issues. From here, you may want to know how to program yourself for the future. What changes would you like to make?

Follow-up: This exercise may be repeated at three-month intervals to see what changes have taken place.

15 Self-Assessment

Level: Teachers.

Background: No matter how good the teaching material is, if the teacher does not feel comfortable with the subject matter, then he or she will not be effective teaching about that subject matter. This is especially true for ethnic studies, or subjects that have to do with racial or ethnic relations. Therefore it is imperative that the teacher find out about his or her feelings with regard to different racial and ethnic groups.

Objective: This self-assessment exercise is designed to assess the teacher's feelings toward various racial and ethnic groups' cultural values.

Materials: You will need a profile sheet. Take a sheet of construction paper and draw four concentric circles around the center, leaving bands wide enough to write on or to put small tabs on. Prepare about 20 or 30 small tabs on which you can write a word or two.

Explanation: This is a free association exercise in which you will be asked to record your emotional response to a series of words, which will be read to you. On the profile sheet are a number of concentric circles and emotional responses are located on them in the following fashion:

1. The central circle is marked "A" and indicates the area of most positive feelings, warmth and closeness, comfort;
2. The second concentric band is marked "B" and indicates the area of ambivalence; there is not much strong feeling either way, positive or negative. However, this is not due to ignorance, just indifference.
3. The next band is marked "C" and indicates the area of negative feelings, intense dislike, hate or rejection; and
4. The space between the last circle and the edges of the paper is marked "D" and indicates the area of ignorance. It indicates lack of knowledge about the subject.

Implementation: A number of terms will be read to you. You will place your tabs at any point on the continuum of the concentric circles, which best expresses your feelings at the moment. It is important that you put down your first reaction.

For our purpose here, we will choose the names of various ethnic groups in the United States. Other terms may be used, which could include cultural values, art objects, books, philosophical concepts, customs, and habits.

Americans
Arabs
Italians
Jews
Koreans
American Indians
Chinese
Africans
African-Americans
Blacks
Japanese
Eskimos
Poles
Asian Indians
Asian Americans
Irish

This exercise can be done either privately, where there will be no discussion of the result, or publicly where there will be an open discussion of the results. In either case it is important that the profile sheet be dated and kept, so that the exercise can be repeated at a later date. You will be able to compare the results. Presumably, as you learn more about a culture or an ethnic group, your feelings and attitudes toward that group will change.

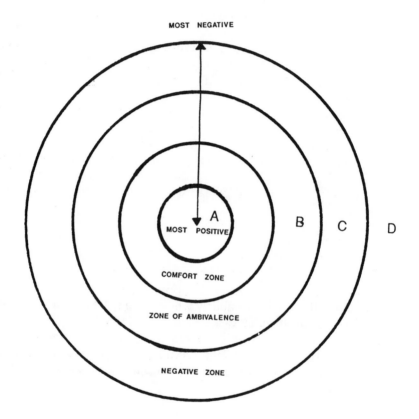

16 Stereotyping Americans

Level: Secondary students and teachers.

Background: We often have stereotypes about others, but we seldom look at the stereotypes about Americans. When we see these stereotypes, we will realize the dangers of stereotyping.

Objective: The students will learn about the dangers of stereotyping by examining stereotypes about Americans.

Implementation: In a class of mixed students, have members of the group write or draw stereotypes about each other's countries. After some discussion about stereotyping, ask members of the group to stereotype Americans. Here are some samples:

> Americans are rich.
> Americans shout a lot.
> Americans wear cowboy boots and eat hotdogs.
> Americans are very aggressive.
> Americans have superficial relationships.
> Americans think only about money.
> Americans are friendly.

There is a grain of truth in each of these statements, but these statements can be equally well applied to people of another culture.

Part III:

Recommendations to the Schools

Developing Resources, Broadening Perspectives

Abraham Resnick

It has not been easy to get Asian American studies introduced into public school systems. An educational system dominated by the majority has hampered the introduction of the history and culture of Asian peoples in America. In order for an effective program to be developed and implemented, it takes the cooperative efforts of parents, teachers, students, and administrators. Problems that must be overcome range from designing a curriculum and choosing a mutually acceptable qualified teacher to finding a suitable time and classroom for the course; from locating financial resources and overcoming resistance from the school board to planning extracurricular activities such as weekend retreats, workshops, and seminars.

In places where Asian American studies programs were developed without the cooperation of the various interested groups, the results have fallen short of expectations. At one school, an Asian American program was developed as part of a multicultural curriculum, but there were few Asian American students. At another, an Asian professional staff developed a program, but without the involvement of Asian American students and parents.

It will take careful planning, preparation, orientation, and lobbying to have Asian American studies, Asian subjects, or even an Asian language taught in the schools. A recent case at the Fort Lee School District (Fort Lee, New Jersey) is a good example. A special 13-member committee was formed to improve relationships between Asian and non-Asian students in the Fort Lee schools. The members of the committee, which consisted of parents, teachers, and the superintendent of the school district, met for one year to plan and implement the program. Not only were curriculum infusion programs introduced, but the PTA also held teas for the parents to get acquainted; the students organized Friendship Clubs and met during lunch hours; and an international field day was held to further interaction between the students.

Nearly two decades earlier, an Asian Task Force was formed in the Berkeley School District (Berkeley, California) to establish an Asian American studies program. There were many meetings and discussions, and the candidate for the position had to face repeated interviews. By the time the teacher was hired, though, it was too late in the year to implement the program. Eventually, a program was developed and several three-day retreats were held to help isolate problems and issues among the Asian American students. As the teacher in charge of these meetings wrote several years later: ". . . the beginning must be recalled if any of us who were involved at that time are to retain a clear under-standing of what we have done, why, and what significance Asian American studies in the Berkeley public school has for us in this city and for other Asian American communities throughout the country. In Berkeley, many Asian people are involved in a dynamic struggle with the politics, economics, and racism of the school system. It is out of this struggle, along with many other struggles, that the future of Asian American people in the United States will be determined." (See, *Counterpoint*, p. 226.)[1]

In this section we will not be concerned with establishing an Asian American curriculum, but rather with a less ambitious goal of develop-ing resources and broadening perspectives. In the following list, a num-ber of educational ideas and suggestions are made for taking the initiative in enhancing learning experiences and instructional resources for improving knowledge and appreciation of Asian students, especially the recent immigrants to America. It must be stressed that the school's professional staff should be in the vanguard of sponsoring methods to foster positive intercultural relationships between Asian and non-Asian youngsters, becoming role models and taking the initiative rather than waiting for problems to develop.

Recommendations in the following areas are made: 1) curriculum improvement for existing courses in Asian studies; 2) development of instructional resources in the library and learning centers; 3) professional initiatives in sponsoring field trips, conferences, and seminars; and 4) school-wide undertakings that involve sister-school exchanges and artists in residence.

CURRICULUM IMPROVEMENT

Courses on Asian and East Asia, aimed at helping students gain an appreciation of cultural diversity, should be established. The courses would recognize the roles Asia and Asian Americans have played in the development of American and world civilization. The program can be implemented in a variety of ways: as a specific course on Asia, as part of an ethnic studies course on multicultural America, as a teaching unit in the social studies curriculum, or as part of a cultural enrichment program. The literature program could offer a course on minority or ethnic writers, featuring Asian American along with African American, Hispanic, and Native American writers.

Often teaching materials on such specific topics are difficult beyond the grade level they will be used for, or simply expensive. But if Asian studies are included in a broader program, teachers can contribute by researching and writing monographs—a short written account of a special subject. The monographs can then be used in tandem with the standard texts.

In addition, many educators realize that Asian languages are rapidly becoming important for commercial purposes and offer business-oriented language courses. But, as was customarily done with European language instruction, schools should make efforts to offer Asian language courses, with a focus on culture as well as business.

RESOURCES AND MATERIALS

Learning materials on Asian subjects—including books, films, videocassettes, maps, and periodicals—should be collected and their circulation encouraged. A special section of the library or learning center can be arranged to showcase the collection. Asian artifacts and crafts should be collected and put on display or used in the classroom.

In addition, a local Asian community can often provide a rich source of information about its ancestral homeland and the experience of acculturation in America. Family and civic organizations, individuals, and the business community can offer insights beyond textbook treatment, and usually are more than willing to help introduce their communities to students. A list of possible resources could be used as a reference directory.

The Asian community or specialists also could serve on a committee to find and evaluate books and other study materials for instructional purposes.

PROFESSIONAL INITIATIVES

A full-time Asian expert, serving as counselor, resource person, and liaison with the Asian community could play an important role in a school with a growing Asian student population. The expert could supplement social studies, art, and literature courses, depending on personal interest and expertise.

Teachers, teacher aides, and administrators also should be encouraged to enroll in Asian studies programs. Fellowships and stipends should be made available, with awards decided on a competitive basis and to institutions where there is a demonstrated need for expertise in Asian cultures. State and local school boards, foundations, endowments, and other contributing agencies could underwrite the programs.

At individual schools, administrators and faculty might sponsor conferences, inservice programs, workshops, seminars, and colloquiums dealing with issues and problems relating to teaching Asian themes or accommodating Asian American students. The meetings should be directed toward educational benefits and outcomes.

Faculty members planning visits to Asian countries during vacation or sabbatical should be encouraged and given incentives to collect instructional materials. School property, such as video cameras and tape recorders, should be made available to the teacher for the trip, and the school can supply the tapes. Photographs, tapes, artifacts, and other materials acquired during the visit would be placed in the school's repository for instructional use.

Funding for such programs, if not available in the district budget, might be obtained from various public and private organizations. Individual districts should be sure that their grant-writers are aware of such possibilities.

SCHOOL-WIDE PROGRAMS AND EVENTS

The school should periodically sponsor special programs and events dealing with Asian topics, commemorations, and issues. These undertakings might include field trips, speakers, films, festivals, plays, pageants, musicals, and sports events.

A parents advisory committee, consisting of parents of Asian ancestry, should be established. The committee would advise school officials about concerns relating to Asian students and Asian study programs. School officials would benefit from the committee by having a recognizable organization that would support and disseminate their initiatives.

Sister school programs can be arranged with schools in many Asian countries, allowing students to correspond and engage in cultural exchange. Some programs even enable students and teacher to live in the foreign country for a time, while American schools host foreign students and teachers.

The "Adopt-a-Student" program arranges for individuals or groups to sponsor a needy child, at a cost of $216 a year. A school could be involved in fund raising for an Asian child. The contact for the program is Jeanne Clark Wood, Children Incorporated, P.O. Box 5381, Richmond, VA 23220 (Telephone: 1–800–538–5381).

CONCLUSION

We have made some suggestions for improving the curriculum. These are only a few possibilities among potentially thousands of programs. Each teacher is encouraged to use his or her own initiative to create and implement programs, which he or she believes are beneficial to the students. Often it is helpful if a teacher works with parents or vice versa. In any case, do not be afraid to take the initiative. We have heard of a case where the parents in cooperation with the teachers created the idea for a month-long "festival" to promote a program in Chinese language and succeeded in persuading the school to give it a try.

NOTE

1. Emma Gee, et al. eds. *Counterpoint: Perspectives on Asian America*, Los Angeles: Asian American Studies Center, UCLA, 1976.

PART IV

Annotated Bibliography

Introduction

Marjorie H. Li and Peter Li

This annotated bibliography of aproximately 400 titles is divided into five sections: Primary Level Books (grades K-6); Intermediate Level Books (grades 7-9); Secondary Level Books (grades 10-12); Works for the General Reader; and Miscellaneous Works. The *Works For the General Reader* section is further divided into five areas dealing with Asia and Asian Americans; Chinese and Chinese Americans; India and Indian Americans; Japan and Japanese Americans; and other Asian groups. The *Miscellaneous Works* section includes ethnic studies, intercultural relations, and general reference works. Works appropriate for more than one category are referenced in each category.

The criteria for selection are accuracy, up-to-date information, interest, and accessibility. Eighty percent of the works were published within the last ten years. A unique feature of this bibliography is that it lists a large number of works of literature, in addition to history, culture, and other more specialized subjects.

Among the many good works included, some need to be singled out for special mention. These works are marked with an asterisk (*) for easy identification. For example,

- James A. Banks, *Teaching Ethnic Studies. Concepts and Strategies* stresses the urgent need to fight racism and prejudice in the schools
- Frank Chin, editor of *Aiiieeeeee! An Anthology on Asian American Writers* has collected an avant-garde sampling of recent writings by Asian American writers

- Emma Gee, editor of *Counterpoint: Perspectives on Asian America* offers an important, comprehensive collection of documents on various aspects of Asian American life
- Tricia Knoll's *Becoming Americans* is one of the most recent intermediate level texts on Asian Americans
- Hyung-chan Kim's *Dictionary of Asian American History* is an important reference works
- Ronald Takaki's *Strangers From a Different Shore* is the most recent and authoritative work on the history of Asian Americans
- Stephan Thernstrom's *The Harvard Encyclopedia of American Ethnic Groups* is a standard, authoritative, and objective reference work with contributions by leading authorities in the field.

Finally, this list has been prepared with school libraries and public libraries in mind. We have not included magazines, articles, dissertations, or many specialized studies.

Primary Level

This section lists 53 titles. Most are works of fiction, including stories, myths, legends, and folktales. Many have excellent illustrations, therefore, the names of the artists are often included. The books are intended for grades K-6. A few originally intended for the upper primary grades (grades 4-6) are included if they are appropriate for younger students as well.

Aruego, Jose. *Juan and the Asuangs*. New York: Charles Scribner, 1970. Story of Juan and his adventures with the *asuangs*, or ghosts and spirits, of the Philippines. It tells how Juan outsmarts the *asuangs* and becomes a hero. Also provides description of other Philippine ghosts and spirits.
—*Philippines/literature/primary*.
Aruego, Jose and Ariane. *A Crocodile's Tale: A Philippine Folk Story*. New York: Scholastic Book Services, 1975. A little boy saves a crocodile's life only to have the animal threaten to eat him.
—*Philippines/literature (folktale)/primary*.
Bennet, Gay. *A Family in Sri Lanka*. Minneapolis: Lerner, 1985. Contemporary family life in Sri Lanka illustrated with photographs of people and activities.
—*India/culture/upper primary*.
Bonnici, Peter. *The Festival*. Illustrated by Lisa Kopper. Minneapolis: Carolrhoda Books, 1985. A young Indian boy, Arjuna, returns to India and experiences the rituals of manhood at the village festival.
—*India/literature/primary*.
Bonnici, Peter. *The First Rains*. Illustrated by Lisa Kopper. Minneapolis: Carolrhoda Books, 1985. Arjuna, a young Indian boy who returns to India, impatiently waits for the first rains of the monsoon season as his family and the villagers prepare for it. Life in modern India.
—*India/literature/primary*.
Bunting, Anne Eve. *The Happy Funeral*. New York: Harper & Row, 1982. A poignant story dealing with a Chinese American girl, Laura. Her beloved grandfather dies, and she attends the funeral. The story illustrates Chinese American customs and traditions.
—*Chinese American/literature/upper primary*.
Cheng, Hou-tien. *The Chinese New Year*. New York: Holt, Rinehart and Winston, 1976. The most important Chinese holidays are described and illustrated with Chinese papercuts.
—*China/culture/primary*.
Chinese Cultural Activities, 2 vols. New York: ARTS, Inc., 1977. Suitable for Chinese bilingual classes and English as a Second Language classes. Also

for Social Studies curriculum through world history or area studies. Activities provide opportunities for intercultural sharing between children of diverse races and languages. Activities include making paper lions, dragons, lanterns, singing folk songs, and performing plays.
—*China/culture/primary.*

Coerr, Eleanor. *Chang's Paper Pony*. New York: Harper & Row, 1988. Set in the 1850s during the gold rush days in San Francisco. Chang, the son of Chinese immigrants, wants a pony but cannot afford one until he meets a friend.
—*Chinese American/literature/primary.*

East/West Activities Kit. 1601 Griffith Park Blvd., Los Angeles, Calif. 90026: Visual Communications/Asian American Studies Central, Inc. Ethnic Understanding Series. Twelve Asian American Activities for grades 3-6. Comes with an accompanying booklet, which gives background information and instructions on the activities.
—*Asian American/culture/primary/intermediate.*

Fisher, Leonard Everett. *The Great Wall*. New York: Macmillan; 1986. A simple retelling of the building of the Great Wall in the third century B.C. by the emperor of the Qin (Chin) dynasty. The illustrations are based on the most recent archeological findings. An accurate and lively presentation. A minor flaw is the use of the term "Mongol" in referring to the people north of the Great Wall. The Mongols did not become known as such until at least 1,000 years later.
—*China/history/primary.*

Fugita, Tamao. *The Boy and the Bird*. New York: John Day, 1971. A young boy releases his pet bird in the forest. He is saddened when the bird does not respond, but happily the bird returns. Story is set in Japan. The beauty of nature is captured in the text and illustrations.
—*Japan/literature/primary.*

Fung, Shiu-ying. *Chinese Children's Games*. New York: ARTS, Inc., 1976. Childhood games that the author played in Hong Kong. Eleven activities are described with illustrations, such as Chinese jump rope, peace on earth, etc.
—*China/culture/activities/primary.*

Fyson, Nance Lui and Richard Greenhill. *A Family in China* (Previously published as Chun Ling in China). Minneapolis: Lerner, 1985. Describes the life of a twelve-year-old from rural northeast People's Republic of China and the ways her childhood is different from her mother's.
—*China/culture/upper primary.*

Goff, Denise. *Early China*. Illustrated by Angus McBride, Karen Johnson, and Terry Dalley. London: Hamilton, 1986. A brief illustrated history of early China.
—*China/history/primary.*

Goom, Bridget. *A Family in Singapore*. Minneapolis: Lerner, 1986. Text and pictures present the life of twelve-year-old Chor Ling and her family, residents of a town in Singapore.

—*Southeast Asia/culture/upper primary.*

Greene, Carol. *Enchantment of the World: Japan.* Chicago: Children's Press, 1983. Describes some of Japan's features in the areas of geography, history, scenic treasures, culture, industry, and people.

—*Japan/history/upper primary.*

Greene, Carol. *Indira Nehru Gandhi, Ruler of India.* Chicago: Children's Press, 1986. Describes how Indira Gandhi followed her family's tradition of fighting politically for India. She became prime minister and was assassinated by her enemies.

—*India/history (biography)/upper primary.*

Havoc In Heaven: Adventures of the Monkey King. Beijing: Foreign Languages Press, 1979. Based on the 16th century novel of fantasy, *Journey To The West,* which portrays a popular folk figure, the Monkey King, who uses his magical powers to frustrate Heaven's attempts to crush him. Illustrated with 84 stills from an animated color cartoon film.

—*China/literature/primary/intermediate.*

Heyer, Marilee. *The Weaving of a Dream. A Chinese Folktale.* New York: Viking Kestrel; 1986. This Chinese folktale is about a widow who wove fine brocades. One day as she sold her work at market, she saw a painting of a glorious palace. Weaving the palace into a brocade, she sought to possess its beauty, but no sooner had she completed it than the wind spirits carried it off. The widow's three sons then made hazardous journeys to retrieve the brocade. Beautiful illustrations.

—*China/literature/primary.*

Horio, Seishi. *The Monkey and the Crab (Saru Kanji).* Union City, Calif.: Heian International, 1985. Mr. Monkey trades his persimmon seed for Mrs. Crab's rice ball. The patient Mrs. Crab plants the seed; after it sprouts and bears fruit, greedy Mr. Monkey kills the crab and takes all the fruit. With the help of a wasp, chestnut, cowpat, and mortar, Mrs. Crab's children take revenge on the monkey.

—*Japan/literature/primary.*

Jacobson, Peter Otto and Preben Sejer Kristensen. *A Family in China.* New York: Bookwright Press, 1986. Text and photographs present the home, work, school, and recreation of the Chen family who live in a city in Guangdong province.

—*China/culture/upper primary.*

Knight, Joan. *Journey to Japan.* New York: Viking Kestrel, 1986. This UNICEF pop-up book teaches young readers about ancient and modern life in Japan. Shows the typical modern home, new technology, old customs, and legends in three-dimensional scenes that bring Japan and its culture to life.

—*Japan/culture/primary.*

Lee, Jeanne M. *Legend of the Milky Way.* New York: Holt, Rinehart & Winston, 1982. Retelling of a famous ancient Chinese tale describing the love be-

tween a shepherd and a heavenly princess.
—*China/literature/primary.*

Lee, Jeanne M. *Legend of the Li River*. New York: Holt, Rinehart and Winston, 1983. An ancient Chinese tale about a sea princess who wishes to lessen the hardship of the poor laborers building the Great Wall of China, and calls upon the Goddess of Mercy for help.
—*China/literature/primary.*

Lim, John. *Merchants of the Mysterious East*. Plattsburgh, N.Y.: Tundra Books, 1981. Text and full-page color pictures recreate the merchants and peddlers of the streets of Singapore. Here the reader meets storytellers, spice grinders, and lantern makers.
—*Southeast Asia/culture/primary/intermediate.*

Louie, Ai Ling. *Yeh Shen: A Cinderella Story from China*. Illustrated by Ed Young. New York: Philomel Books, 1982. An ancient Chinese fairy tale that predates the Western story of Cinderella by 1,000 years. Beautifully illustrated by Ed Young, an author/artist who grew up in China.
—*China/literature/primary.*

Luenn, Nancy. *The Dragon Kite*. Illustrated by Michael Hague. New York: Harcourt Brace Jovanovich, 1982. Ishikawa, a Robin Hood figure of late seventeenth-century Japan, schemes with a magnificent dragon kite to steal a golden dolphin. After accomplishing the deed, he turns the red and silver kite, which seems to have come alive, free. Later the dragon kite returns to rescue him. Hague's illustrations captures the costume, architecture, and history of seventeenth-century Japan.
—*Japan/literature/primary.*

McKillop, Beth. *China, 1400BC-AD1911*. New York: Franklin Watts, 1988. Briefly traces the history of China from ancient times to the present.
—*China/history/primary/intermediate.*

Newton, Patricia Montgomery. *The Five Sparrows: A Japanese Folktale*. New York: Atheneum, 1982. When a kind old woman is richly rewarded for nursing a wounded sparrow back to health, a greedy neighbor attempts to emulate the old woman and brings trouble upon herself and her family.
—*Japan/literature (folktale)/primary.*

Okawa, Essei. *The Fisherman and the Turtle (Urashima Taro)*. Union City, Calif.: Heian International, 1985. A young fisherman saves a turtle. The grateful turtle invites the fisherman to its Sea Palace, where he is entertained by the Sea Princess. Time passes quickly. When the fisherman returns to his village, he discovers that he has already turned into an old man.
—*Japan/literature/primary.*

Robertson, Dorothy Lewis. *Fairy Tales From the Philippines*. New York: Dodd, Mead and Co., 1971. A collection of traditional fairy tales. Included are some unusual characters such as the *tiyanak*, or monster. These fairy tales have a lot in common with those of other languages but also have differences that make them unique, such as unusual settings and personalities, providing the readers with an insight into the customs and be-

liefs of the people.
—Philippines/literature (folktales)/primary.
Sabin, Louis. *Ancient China.* Illustrated by Hal Frenck. Mahwah, N.J.: Troll Associates, 1985. Briefly traces the history of early China including the T'ang and Sung dynasties.
—China/history/primary.
Sakade, Florence. *Japanese Children's Stories.* Rutland, Vt.: Charles E. Tuttle, 1972. A collection of 15 Japanese traditional stories that have captivated the hearts of children through generations. Other titles in the series by the same author include *Kintaro's Adventures and Other Japanese Children's Stories, Little One-inch and Other Japanese Children's Favorite Stories, Peach Boy and Other Japanese Children's Favorite Stories.*
—Japan/literature/primary.
Say, Allen. *The Bicycle Man.* New York: Houghton, Mifflin, 1982. Two American soldiers on a borrowed bicycle do amazing tricks for the school day festivities in a small village in occupied Japan.
—Japan/liteature/primary.
Scarsbrook, Ailsa and Alan. *A Family in Pakistan.* Minneapolis: Lerner, 1985. Contemporary life in Pakistan illustrated by photographs of people and activities.
—Pakistan/India/culture/intermediate.
Schloat, G. Warren, Jr. *Junichi: Boy of Japan.* New York: Alfred A. Knopf, 1964. Follows a twelve-year-old Japanese boy and his family through their daily routines.
Japan/culture/upper primary.
Schloat, G. Warren, Jr. *Uttam, A Boy of India.* New York: Knofp, 1963. Photographs and text describe family life, village chores, religious, and traditional customs in a farming village in India.
—India/culture/primary.
Seros, Kathleen. *Sun and Moon: Fairy Tales From Korea.* Elizabeth, N.J., Seoul, Korea: Hollym International, 1982. Contains seven stories skillfully adapted by the author. The world of Korean fairytales is populated by malevolent giants, whimsical goblins, sly rabbits, and greedy tigers.
—Korea/literature/primary/intermediate.
Shibano, Tamizo. *The Old Man Who Made the Trees Bloom (Hanasaka Jijii).* Union City, Calif.: Heian International, 1985. A kind old couple and their dog, Shiro, live next door to a greedy old couple. Shiro brings good fortune to his master and mistress in gratitude for their kindness to him. When the greedy old couple tries to imitate their good neighbors, misfortune is the result.
—Japan/literature/primary.
Spellman, John W. *The Beautiful Blue Jay and Other Tales of India.* Illustrated by Jerry Piukney. Boston: Little, Brown & Co., 1967. Contains 25 stories, which have been gathered from all over India. Most have never appeared in print before. These stories are not based on classic tales, but are stories that mothers tell their children in India today. Well written

and finely illustrated; collected and edited by the author.
—*India/literature/primary/intermediate.*

Surat, Michele Maria. *Angel Child, Dragon Child.* Illustrated by Vo-Dinh Mai. Milwaukee: Raintree Publishers, 1983. Ut, a Vietnamese girl attending school in the United States, is lonely for her mother who was left behind in Vietnam. Ut makes a new friend who presents her with a wonderful gift.
—*Vietnamese Americans/fiction/primary.*

Thompson, Brenda and Cynthia Overbeck. *The Great Wall of China.* Minneapolis: Learner, 1977. Tells why and how this 1,500-mile historical structure in China was planned and built.
—*China/history/primary.*

Tigwell, Tony. *A Family in India.* Minneapolis: Lerner, 1985. Contemporary life in India illustrated with photographs of people and activities.
—*India/culture/intermediate.*

Uchida, Yoshiko. *The Birthday Visitor.* New York: Charles Scribner, 1975. A well-illustrated story of a Japanese American family in the 1930s.
—*Japanese American/literature/primary.*

Uchida, Yoshiko. *The Sea of Gold and Other Tales from Japan.* Illustrated by Marianne Yamaguchi. Boston: Gregg Press, 1980. Contains 12 stories adapted by Yoshiko Uchida, a gifted Japanese American writer of books for young adults. Covers a wide range and a host of colorful characters—a long-nosed goblin, a shrewd monkey, a formidable river ogre, and a terrible black snake.
—*Japan/literature (folktales)/primary.*

Uyeda, Frances and Jeannie Sasaki. *Fold, Cut and Say the Japanese Way.* Seattle: Uyeda Sasaki Art, 1975. A Japanese activity book for young children.
—*Japan/culture/primary.*

Vuong, Lynette Dyer. *The Brocaded Slipper and other Vietnamese Tales.* Illustrated by Vo-Dinh Mai. New York: J.B. Lippincott, 1982. Five stories reflecting universal folklore themes, including "The Brocaded Slipper," "Master Frog," and others. Well illustrated.
—*Southeast Asia/literature/primary/intermediate.*

Wallace, Ian. *Chin Chiang and the Dragon's Dance.* New York: Atheneum, 1984. A young Chinese boy has long dreamed of dancing the dragon's dance, but when the first day of the Year of the Dragon arrives, he is sure he will shame his family and bring bad luck to everyone so he runs away and hides. With beautiful watercolor illustrations by the author.
—*Chinese Americans/literature/primary.*

Xu Li. *Trouble on Black Wind Mountain* (Monkey Series). Beijing: Foreign Languages Press, 1985. One of eight in a series of 34 projected picture books based on a sixteenth-century novel of fantasy, *Journey to the West,* a story rich in tales about demons and monsters who try to stop a Buddhist monk from reaching India to fetch scriptures back to China. This volume tells of how Monk Xuanzang's cassock is stolen by the Black Bear Spirit when Monkey shows it off at a monastery. Illustrated by excellent colored cartoons. Others in the series include: *The Beginnings of Monkey, Monkey Makes Havoc in Heaven, Monkey's Conversion, The Coming of Pig, Friar Sand Joins the Pilgrims, Stealing the Magic Fruit, The Yellow Robe Monster*.

—*China/literature/primary/intermediate.*

Yagawa, Sumiko. *The Crane Wife.* Translated by Katherine Paterson. Illustrated by Suekicki Akaba. New York: William Morrow, 1981. A retelling of one of Japan's best loved folktales. A hauntingly tragic story of a crane that changes herself into a woman to repay a poor farmer for his kindness to her. But the poor farmer is overtaken by greed and he loses his crane wife. The story has been made into plays, movies, and even an opera.

—*Japan/literature/primary.*

Yashima, Taro. *Umbrella.* New York: Viking, 1958. A Japanese American girl is the subject of this book which conveys the excitement and pleasure of a small child with her first umbrella and red boots.

—*Japanese Americans/literature/primary.*

Young, Ed. *High on a Hill: A Book of Chinese Riddles.* New York: Collins, 1980. A lively selection of authentic Chinese riddles on the traditional themes of animals and people. The book is beautifully illustrated with the riddles printed in both English and Chinese characters.

—*China/culture/primary.*

Intermediate Level

The 79 items listed in this section are intended for grades 7-9. Most of the books at this level concern social studies: culture and history. There are fewer works of fiction than in the primary section, but there are two outstanding fiction writers for young adults who are worthy of note: Yoshida Uchida, who writes about Japanese American youths, and Laurence Yep, who writes about Chinese American youths. Lerner Publications and Julian Messner are both major publishers of texts at the intermediate level. *Global Insights: People and Cultures* is a noteworthy text published recently by Merrill Publishing Co. It deals with seven cultural areas, including China, Japan, and India.

Bagai, Leona B. *The East Indians and Pakistanis In America*. Minneapolis: Lerner, 1972. One of a series designed to encourage understanding of the many national, social, and ethnic groups that together make up the population of the United States.
   —*Asian Indian Americans/history/intermediate.*
Beach, Milo Cleveland. *The Adventures of Rama*. Washington, D.C.: Freer Gallery of Art, 1985. The adventures of a supernatural monkey from India's classic sixth century B.C. epic poem, The Ramayana. The illustrations are from a sixteenth-century manuscript in the Freer Gallery of Art.
   —*India/literature/intermediate.*
Blackwood, Alan. *Spotlight on the Rise of Modern China*. Hove, England: Wayland, 1986. Briefly traces the history of modern China up to 1985.
   —*China/history/intermediate.*
Bocca, Geoffrey. *The Philippines: America's Forgotten Friend*. New York: Parents Magazine, 1974. A history of the Philippines, stressing its political development and its tragic struggle in World War II.
   —*Philippines/history/intermediate.*
Bolitho, Harold. *Meiji Japan*. Minneapolis: Lerner, 1980. Examines the dramatic changes that occurred in Japan after diplomatic and economic relations were established with the West after the arrival of Admiral Perry in 1853.
   —*Japan/History/Intermediate.*
Bonham, Frank. *The Burma Rifles*. New York: Crowell, 1960. Jerry Harada is a Japanese American of draft age at the time of Pearl Harbor and suffers from the hatred of his neighbors. He and his family are interned in a camp. Later he enlists in the U.S. Navy.
   —*Japanese Americans/literature/intermediate.*
Bosse, Malcolm. *Ganesh*. New York: Crowell Junior Books, 1981. Ganesh—Jeffrey Moore—is the son of Americans who adopted Hinduism as their re-

ligion. He is Indian in culture, American in parentage. The death of his
father marks the end of his place in the Indian village of his birth. Now
he must live with his aunt in the American midwest and make an adjustment.

—*Indian Americans/literature/intermediate.*

Buck, Pearl S. *The Big Wave.* Illustrated with prints by Hiroshige and Hokusai.
New York: John Day, 1948. Deals with Japanese culture, socialization
processes, and social situations. Good illustrations with examples of ancient Japanese art. One of the perennial favorites.

—*Japan/literature/intermediate.*

Carlson, Dale. *The Beggar King of China.* New York: Atheneum, 1971. The story
of Chu Yuan-chang, commonly called the Beggar King because he was
the son of a poor farmer. Later he led a band of rebels, overthrew the
Yuan dynasty, and established himself as the Emperor of the Ming dynasty in 1368.

—*China/history/intermediate.*

Chang, Heidi. *Elaine, Mary Lewis, and the Frogs.* New York: Crown, 1988.Chi-
nese American Elaine Chow feels like an outcast after moving to a small
town in Iowa, until she shares a new friendship and a science project
with a girl who is strongly interested in frogs.

—*Chinese-Americans/literature/intermediate.*

Chun, Shinae and Patricia Donegan. *A Passage Through the Hermit Kingdom.*
Deerfield, Ill.: Asia Press, 1980. This resource book about Korea is di-
vided into topical sections and covers ancient Korea and modern South
Korea.

—*Korea/History/Intermediate.*

Crew, Linda. *Children of the River.* New York: Delacorte Press, 1989. A 17-year-
old girl, Sundara, having fled Cambodia four years earlier to escape the
Khmer Rouge army, is torn between remaining faithful to her own people and enjoying life in her Oregon high school as a ":regular" American
girl.

—*Southeast Asian Americans/literature/intermediate.*

Daley, William. *The Chinese Americans.* New York: Chelsea House, 1987. Discusses the history, culture, and religion of the Chinese, factors encouraging their emigration, and their acceptance as an ethnic group in North
American. With an introductory essay by Daniel Patrick Moynihan.

—*Chinese Americans/history/intermediate.*

Davidson, Judith. *Japan: Where East Meets West.* Minneapolis: Dillon Press,
1983. This textbook is an introduction to the history and culture of
Japan, including a discussion of the Japanese in the United States. It includes appendices explaining *hiragana* writing symbols and how to
make a kimono.

—*Japan/history/intermediate.*

Dowdell, Dorothy and Joseph. *The Chinese Helped Build America.* New York: Julian Messner, 1972. A young Chinese peasant leaves his native China to
travel to the gold fields of California, where he works and lives at min-

ing and railroad building sites. Later he marries, opens a laundry, is harassed by whites, and moves to a more pleasant life in New York City. The last part of the book explains the life of modern-day Chinese Americans. Many drawings and photographs.
—*Chinese Americans/history/secondary.*

Dowdell, Dorothy and Joseph. *The Japanese Helped Build America.* Illustrated by Len Ebert. New York: Julian Messner, 1970. Interspersed with photographs and illustrations, this book tells the story of the Japanese emigration to America from 1870 to the present. It describes the reasons they emigrated and their contributions in the arts, architecture, and agriculture. Factual accounts of the Japanese in America illustrate their customs, festivals, and prejudices they faced in America, and their forced evacuation into camps during World War II.
—*Japanese Americans/history/intermediate.*

Dunster, Jack. *China and Mao Zedong.* New York: Lerner in cooperation with Cambridge University Press, 1982. Describes in simple language Mao's rise to power in the newly formed Communist party, the struggle with the Kuomingtang and China's transformation into a Communist society. Also covers changes that have taken place since Mao's death.
—*China/history/intermediate.*

Filstrup, Chris and Janie. *China: From Emperors to Communes.* Minneapolis: Dillon Press, 1983. This textbook presents facts about Chinese history, art, traditions, social life, and recreation. Includes a chapter on Chinese Americans, a glossary, and a map of China.
—*China/history/intermediate.*

Fritz, Jean. *Homesick, My Own Story.* Illustrated with drawings and photographs by Margot Tomes. New York: G. P. Putnam, 1982. The author's childhood in China during the turbulent 1920s and her nostalgia for the United States, a homeland she has imagined but never seen, are the main themes in the book. This is one of five "honor books" of the Newbery Medal Award.
—*China/literature/intermediate.*

Gilson, Jamie. *Hello, My Name is Scrambled Eggs.* New York: Simon & Schuster, 1985. When his folks host a Vietnamese family that has come to settle in their town, Harvey enjoys Americanizing 12-year-old Tuan.
—*Vietnamese Americans/literature/intermediate.*

Hantula, James Neil, et al. *Global Insights: People and Cultures.* Columbus, Ohio: Merrill, 1987. An innovative intermediate text on the people and cultures of eight important cultural centers of the world: Africa, China, Japan, India, Latin America, Middle East, the Soviet Union, and Western Europe. Each unit, chapter, and section has helpful review questions, reading skills development exercises, explorations, insights on people, and case studies, which all help to integrate the knowledge into the overall view of the culture. Includes many color photos, diagrams, charts, and maps. A well-thought out text that challenges traditional stereotypes.

—China/Japan/India/history/intermediate/secondary.

Harmon, Betty. *The Moon Rock Heist.* Austin, Tex.: Eakin Press, 1988. Joseph
and his Vietnamese American friend, Huy, investigate the disappear-
ance of a moon rock loaned by NASA to their high school in Galveston
Bay.
—Vietnamese Americans/literature/intermediate.

Havoc in Heaven: Adventures of the Monkey King. (For full citation, see Primary
Section.)

Howard, Ellen. *Her Own Song.* New York: Atheneum, 1988. When her adop-
tive father is hospitalized after an accident, Mellie is befriended by
Geem-Wah, owner of a Chinese laundry, who holds the key to the
events surrounding Mellie's birth 11 years before.
—Chinese Americans/literature/intermediate.

"India, a Teacher's Guide," in *Focus on Asian Studies.* New York: The Asia Society, 1985. Prepared for the special occasion of the "Festival of India" year
1985-86. The guide uses an interdisciplinary approach and is focused
with special chapters on "Contemporary Society," "Identity," "Perception," and "Expression of Reality, Values, and Decision Making." Each
chapter has a section of background readings, activities, and a section of
student readings that are the key to the classroom activities. An excellent guide.
—India/culture/intermediate.

Irwin, Hadley. *Kim/Kimi.* New York: Viking Penguin, 1988. Despite a warm relationship with her mother, stepfather, and half brother, 16-year-old Kim
feels the need to find answers about the Japanese American father she
never knew.
—Japanese Americans/literature/intermediate.

Jaffrey, Madhur. *Seasons of Splendour: Tales, Myths and Legends of India.* New
York: Atheneum, 1985. A collection of 23 stories arranged according to
the season's festivals. Each story is prefaced by an introduction in which
the author recalls anecdotes from her childhood to give the stories a personal touch. Storytelling was an important part of her family life.
—India/literature/intermediate.

Johnson, Sylvia A. *Silkworms.* Photos by Isao Kishida. Minneapolis: Lerner
(Lerner Natural Science Books), 1982. Explains the life cycle of the silkworm and how people use silk thread to make fabric. The stages of a
silkworm moth's development are shown in detailed color photographs.
—Asia/culture/intermediate.

Jones, Claire. *The Chinese in America.* Minneapolis: Lerner (In America Series),
1972. Discusses the reasons for immigration of the Chinese to the United
States, their problems here, and their contributions to American life. Illustrated with numerous black-and-white photographs. Designed to encourage understanding of the many national, social, and ethnic groups
that make up the population of the United States.
—Chinese Americans/history/intermediate.

Jue, David. *Chinese Kites: How to Make and Fly Them*. Rutland, Vt.: Charles E. Tuttle, 1967. An attractive book describing various types of kites with instructions on how to make them. Traditional stories and customs relating to Chinese kites are also mentioned.
—*China/culture/intermediate*.

Klass, David. *The Atami Dragons*. New York: Scribner, 1984. Jerry "Boomer" Sanders goes to Japan with his father and sister. Loneliness and culture shock hit him hard until he joins the Atami Dragons, the local high school baseball team.
—*Japanese Americans/literature/intermediate*.

Lawson, Don. *The Long March: Red China Under Chairman Mao*. New York: Crowell Junior Books, 1983. An account of the Long March and of the political, social, and military events of the period during the 1930s.
—*China/history/intermediate*.

Leathers, Noel L. *The Japanese in America*. Minneapolis: Lerner (In America Books), 1982. Designed to encourage understanding of the many national, social, and ethnic groups that make up the population of the United States.
—*Japanese Americans/history/intermediate*.

Lee, Calvin. *Chinatown, U.S.A.* Garden City, N.Y.: Doubleday, 1965. The author, a second-generation Chinese American from New York, traces the history and development of Chinatowns in the United States. The Chinese culture and way of life are presented in a popular style.
—*Chinese Americans/history/intermediate*.

Lord, Bette Bao. *In the Year of the Boar and Jackie Robinson*. New York: Harper & Row, 1984. This is a poignant and often outrageously humorous story about a Chinese girl, Shirley Temple Wong, who comes to Brooklyn in 1947, does not know English, and has problems adjusting to a new country. Then a miracle happens; she discovers baseball and the Brooklyn Dodgers.
—*Chinese Americans/literature/intermediate*.

Macmillan, Diane. *My Best Friend, Duc Tran: Meeting a Vietnamese-American Family*. New York: J. Messner, 1987. An American boy's friendship with a Vietnamese American boy and his family introduces him to the holidays, customs, foods, and family events of their culture.
—*Vietnamese Americans/literature/intermediate*.

Martin, Rafe. *The Hungry Tigress and Other Traditional Asian Tales*. Illustrated by Richard Wehrman. Boulder, Colo./London: Shambhala, 1984. Contains 20 stories, or *Jataka* tales, that is, tales of Buddha's earlier births. Retold in a lively manner by the prize-winning professional storyteller Rafe Martin. These stories tell of respect and love for all living things, courage, perseverance, good humor, and faith. They delight and entertain as well as instruct.
—*India/literature/intermediate*.

McCarty, Toni. *The Skull in the Snow, and Other Folktales*. New York: Delacorte Press, 1981. These folktales highlight heroines and include Chinese, Japanese, and Pakistani tales.
—*Asia/literature (folktales)/intermediate*.

McCunn, Ruthanne Lum. *An Illustrated History of the Chinese in America*. San Francisco: Design Enterprises of San Francisco, 1979. A readable account of the Chinese in the United States, which focuses on their struggle for acceptance by the white population and their contributions to the development of their new country. Reveals how the Chinese were discriminated against from the beginning of their immigration in the 1850s to 1943 when the Exclusion Act of 1883 was repealed. Illustrated with photographs, drawings, and cartoons.
—*Chinese Americans/history/intermediate*.

McKillop, Beth. *China, 1400BC–AD1911*. (For full citations, see Primary Section.)

McLenighan, Val jean. *China, A History to 1949*. Chicago: Childrens Press, 1983. The history of China to 1949.
—*China/history/intermediate*.

Meltzer, Milton. *The Chinese Americans*. New York: Thomas Y. Crowell, 1980. A straightforward lively account of the Chinese in America focusing on railroad building, gold mining, and the struggle against prejudice and racism. By a noted social historian, the book tells us that the first arrivals found low wages, ridicule, abuse, and violence instead of gold.
—*Chinese Americans/history/intermediate*.

Namioka, Lensey. *Who's Hu?* New York: Vanguard Press, 1980. Set in the 1950s, this story tells of a Chinese American girl Emma Hu, who feels out of place in her community because she is caught between two cultures. Her parents ask: Why date Americans? How dare you go out on an unchaperoned date? Why bother with a prom? The book not only explores the issue of nationality and prejudice, but also shows how girls view themselves, and how they come to grips with disparate perspectives.
—*Chinese Americans/literature/intermediate*.

Norton, James H.K. *South Asia*. Guilford, Conn.: Dushkin Publishing Group, 1984. Discusses the region of South Asia from the perspective of third world societies and cultures in transition. Focuses on the problems of new nations such as Afganistan, Pakistan, India, Nepal, Bhutan, Sri Lanka, and Bangladesh. Investigates the ways in which traditional norms and modern forms interact, especially as the nations struggle with issues of economic development.
—*India/history/intermediate*.

Paterson, Katherine. *Park's Quest*. New York: Puffin books, 1989. Eleven-year-old Park makes some startling discoveries when he travels to his grandfather's farm in Virginia to learn about his father who died in the Vietnam War.
—*Vietnamese Americans/literature/intermediate*.

Patterson, Wayne and Hyung-chan Kim. *The Koreans in America*. Minneapolis: Lerner (In America Series), 1977. An objective survey of the origins of Korean civilization, immigration to America, life and treatment in America, and contributions to American life. Designed to encourage understanding of the many national, social, and ethnic groups that helped build America.
   —*Korean Americans/history/intermediate.*
Perrin, Linda. *Coming to America: Immigrants From the Far East*. New York: Delacorte, 1980. Discusses four immigrant groups to the United States: Chinese, Japanese, Filipino, and Vietnamese. A readable account; many quotations from primary sources add life to the narrative.
   —*Asian Americans/history/intermediate.*
Pitts, Forest Ralph, ed. *Japan*. Grand Rapids: Fideler Co., 1981. A social studies textbook, which includes the geography, history, people, culture, and economy of Japan.
   —*Japan/history/intermediate.*
Rawding, F.W. *The Buddha*. Minneapolis: Lerner, 1979. Life of Prince Siddartha Gotama, the Buddha, is told here against the background of the early history of India. The book includes an account of the legends and mythology surrounding the Buddha and explains the doctrines of Buddhism in simple terms.
   —*Asia/culture/intermediate.*
Rawding, F.W. *Gandhi and the Struggle for India's Independence*. Minneapolis, MN: Lerner, 1982. Recounts the inspiring life of Mohandas Gandhi—a twentieth century political and religious prophet who died for his beliefs. Gandhi's leadership was characterized as forceful, charismatic, yet loving.
   —*India/history/intermediate.*
Rawding, F.W. *The Rebellion in India, 1857*. New York: Cambridge University Press, 1977. An account of the establishment of the English East India Company, the growth of British power in India, and the mutiny of 1857 in which the Indian soldiers in the Bengal Army revolted against their British officers.
   —*India/history/intermediate.*
Reit, Seymour. *Rice Cakes and Paper Dragons*. New York: Dodd, Mead & Co., 1973. Text and photographs introduce a girl of Chinatown in New York City, her family, and their celebration of Chinese New Year.
   —*Chinese Americans/literature/intermediate.*
Rutledge, Paul. *The Vietnamese in America*. Minneapolis: Lerner, 1987. Surveys Vietnamese immigration to the United Sates and discusses the contributions made by the Vietnamese in various areas of American life.
   —*Vietnamese Americans/historical/intermediate.*
Scarsbrook, Ailsa and Alan. *A Family in Pakistan*. Lerner, 1985. (For full citation, see Primary Section.)
Schwartz, Rudolph, Harold Hammond, and Adriane Ruggiero. *Japan, Korea, Taiwan: History, Culture, People*. New York: Globe Book, 1981. Provides

an overview of the role that thousands of years of tradition have played in shaping Japan, Korea, and Taiwan.
—*Japan/Korea/Taiwan/history/intermediate.*

Seros, Kathleen. *Sun and Moon. Fairy Tales from Korea.* (For full citation, see Primary Section.)

Smith, Datus C., Jr. *The Land and People of Indonesia.* New York: Lippincott Junior Books (Portraits of Nations), 1983. Provides an introduction to Indonesia, covering its history, geography, politics, people, and culture.
—*Southeast Asia/history/intermediate.*

Spellman, John W. *The Beautiful Blue Jay and Other Tales of India.* Illustrated by Jerry Piukney. Boston: Little, Brown & Co., 1967. (For full citation, see Primary Section.)

Sung, Betty Lee. *The Chinese in America.* New York: MacMillan, 1972. A sympathetic portrait of the Chinese in America by a Chinese American sociologist, who has drawn upon her own experience to describe customs, foods, festivals, and lifestyles. The author is one of the pioneers in the study of the Chinese in America. Lively as well as informative.
—*Chinese Americans/history/intermediate.*

Telemaque, Eleanor Wong. *It is Crazy to stay Chinese in Minnesota.* Nashville, Tenn.: Thomas Nelson Inc., 1986. A fictionalized account of a girl growing up in a small town in Minnesota where her parents run a Chinese restaurant. They are the only Chinese family in town in the 1950s. She, as the only daughter, waits on tables, tends the cash register, and moons over movie magazines. She wants to be an American, like everybody else in school or outside the restaurant. Torn between Eastern and Western cultures, the author presents a lighthearted glimpse of her Midwest girlhood struggles.
—*Chinese Americans/literature/intermediate.*

Tigwell, Tony. *A Family in India.* (For full citation, see Primary Section.)

Turnbull, Stephen. *Warlords of Japan.* London: Sampson Low, 1979. This book tells of the life and role of the samurai in classical Japan from the twelfth to the nineteenth century. Richly illustrated with painting and photographs.
—*Japan/history/intermediate.*

Uchida, Yoshiko. *The Best Bad Thing.* New York: Atheneum, 1983. A Japanese American girl, Rinko, has to spend the last month of summer vacation helping Mrs. Hata, who eats garlic for breakfast and says things that do not make sense. But Rinko soon learns the reasons for her eccentricities and how strong she really is. Second-generation Japanese American's perspective on the "strange ways" of first-generation Japanese Americans.
—*Japanese Americans/literature/intermediate.*

Uchida, Yoshida. *A Jar of Dreams.* New York: Atheneum, 1981. Being Japanese in California during the Depression was hard. Fortunately Aunt Waka arrives from Japan for a summer visit and gives courage and inspiration

to the family. A warm, touching, and very real story about the life of a Japanese family during difficult times.
—*Japanese Americans/literature/intermediate.*

Uchida, Yoshiko. *Journey to Topaz.* Abridged by Diane Durston. Annotated by Masaru Amafugi. Kyoto: Yamaguchi Shoten, 1984. This autobiographical novel relates the daily life in a relocation camp and the way the Japanese Americans endured their upheaval with quiet dignity. A story of a Japanese American family imprisoned behind barbed wires in the United Sates during World War II.
—*Japanese Americans/literature/intermediate.*

Uchida, Yoshiko. *Samurai of Gold Hill.* New York: Charles Scribner, 1972. A boy escapes from Japan and becomes a part of the first group of Japanese to settle in the United States.
—*Japanese Americans/literature/intermediate.*

Vexler, Robert and William Cowan. *China: History, Culture, People.* New York: Globe Book, 1981. An overview of China, past and present for young adults. Historical perspective is given to enrich understanding of China's achievements and current concerns.
—*China/history/intermediate.*

Vuong, Lynette Dyner. *The Brocaded Slipper and Other Vietnamese Tales.* (For full citation, see Primary Section.)

Wartski, Maureen Crane. *A Boat to Nowhere.* Philadelphia: Westminster Press, 1980. The story of Mei and her family, who left their home in Vietnam and became boat people, risking the perils of pirates, storms, sickness, and starvation to find a land where they could be free. A moving tragedy of the Vietnamese people, and the triumph of their spirit over intense adversity.
—*Vietnamese Americans/literature/intermediate.*

Wartski, Maureen Crane. *A Long Way From Home.* Philadelphia: Westminster Press, 1980. The story of three Vietnamese children, Mai, Loc, and Kien, and their adjustment to American life, especially for Kien who seemed to be constantly running into trouble. He finally realizes that he must face up to the problems instead of running away from them.
—*Vietnamese Americans/literature/intermediate.*

Weston, Reiko. *Cooking the Japanese Way.* Minneapolis: Lerner, 1983. Step-by-step instructions for sukiyaki, teriyaki, and other Japanese main dishes, side dishes, soups, appetizers, and desserts. Also describes some special ingredients used in Japanese dishes, how to set a Japanese table, and how to eat with chopsticks.
—*Japan/culture/intermediate.*

William, Kate. *Out of Reach.* Lakeville, Conn.: Grey Castle Press, 1989. Jade Wu, a talented dancer, accepts a role in a show despite the objections of her traditional father.
—*Chinese Americans/literature/intermediate.*

Wong, Don and Irene Dea Collier. *Chinese Americans Past and Present. A Collection of Chinese American Readings and Learning Activities.* 1 Waverly Place,

San Francisco, Calif. 94108: Association of Chinese Teachers, 1977. An intermediate-level text used in the schools tò give an honest and accurate picture of Chinese Americans. Contains stories about the experiences of the Chinese in America from the late 1800s to the present day. Written in the form of letters and stories.
—*Chinese Americans/history/intermediate.*

Wriggins, Sally Hovey. *White Monkey King. A Chinese Fable.* New York: Pantheon Books, 1977. A lively retelling of the sixteenth century novel of fantasy Journey to the West about a supernatural monkey and three disciples who accompany their Buddhist Master Tripitaka to obtain sacred scriptures from India. One of the favorite classic Chinese stories.
—*China/literature/intermediate.*

Xu Li. *Trouble on Black Wind Mountain* (Monkey Series). Beijing: Foreign Languages Press, 1985. (For full citation, see Primary Section.)

Yep, Laurence. *Child of the Owl.* New York: Harper & Row, 1977. "San Francisco's Chinatown of the early '60s is the testing ground for 12-year-old Casey who, in finding her roots, forfeits her faith in her compulsive gambler father."—*School Library Journal.* Best Children's Book of 1977.
—*Chinese Americans/literature/intermediate.*

Yep, Laurence. *Dragonwings.* New York: Harper & Row, 1975. Windrider and his son, Moon Shadow, build a flying machine in "an unusual historical novel, unique in its perspective on the Chinese in America and its portrayal of early twentieth-century San Francisco , including the Earthquake, from an immigrant's viewpoint."—*School Library Journal* Outstanding Children's Book of 1975.
—*Chinese Americans/literature/intermediate.*

Yep, Laurence. *Sea Glass.* New York: Harper & Row, 1979. "Eighth grader Craig Chin suffers from a common adolescent malady: he cannot meet the exacting demands of his first generation Chinese American father. After moving from San Francisco's Chinatown to a suburban community, Craig . . . must ward off his two well-off cousins' insults about his weight, his athletic ineptitude, and his refusal to deny his heritage. . . ." School Library Journal.
—*Chinese Americans/literature/intermediate.*

Yu, Ling. *Cooking the Chinese Way.* Minneapolis: Lerner Publications, 1982. Basic Chinese cooking becomes simple when readers follow the instructions for appetizers, soups, rice, main dishes, vegetables, and desserts.
—*China/culture/intermediate.*

Secondary Level

Following are 44 titles intended for students in grades 10-12. Students at this level should also consult works at the general reader level. There are a number of literary works that should be of interest to secondary school students: Jeanne Houston's *Farewell to Manzanar*, John Okada's *No-No Boy*, Louis Chu's *Eat a Bowl of Tea*, Maxine Hong Kingston's *Woman Warrior*, and Indian American writer Bharati Mukherjee's *Darkness*.

Beneger, John, Heidi Hursh, Jacquelyn Johnson, and Huang Teh-Ming. *Changing Images of China*. Denver: Center for Teaching International Relations, University of Denver, 1986. A collection of activities exploring relations between the United States and China.
   —*China/culture/activities/secondary*.
Bernstein, Gail Lee. *Haruko's World: A Japanese Farm Woman and Her Community*. Stanford: Stanford University Press, 1983. A readable and enjoyable book on rural Japanese women as seen through the life of a farm woman, Haruko. It describes the relationships between family and community, family and school, and the effects of mechanization of agriculture on the family. May be read in conjunction with John Nathan's film *Farm Song*.
   —*Japan/culture/secondary/general*.
Boyd, James W. and Loren W. Crabtree. *Discovering India and China: The Lion and the Dragon*. Portland, Me.: J. Weston Walch, 1979. An introductory text with study questions, projects, and additional readings following each chapter. Provides basic information on the culture, history, social life, and customs of the two countries.
   —*China/India/history/secondary*.
Buck, Pearl S. *The Hidden Flower*. New York: John Day, 1952. This novel presents an important historical perspective on racism in America by examining the life of Josui, a young Japanese woman who marries an American soldier and emigrates to the United States.
   —*Japanese Americans/literature/secondary*.
Bulosan, Carlos. *America Is in the Heart: A Personal History*. Seattle: University of Washington Press, 1981. A classic literary autobiography of a Filipino laborer who came to America as a young man. Bulosan describes the hardships, despair, and horrors experienced by a large number of Pilipino migrant workers. Highly moving in its discussion of the impact of racism on Bulosan's life.
   —*Filipino Americans/literature/secondary/general*.

Bush, Richard C. *Religion in China*. Allen Niles, Ill.: Argus Communications (Major World Religions Series), 1977. Probably the best available introduction to the subject.
—*China/culture/secondary*.

Cavanna, Betty. *Jenny Kimura*. New York: Morrow, 1964. This novel examines the problem of personal identity and the effects of an interracial marriage on a teenage girl who is half American and half Japanese.
—*Japanese Americans/literature/secondary*.

Chu, Daniel and Samuel Chu. *Passage to the Golden Gate: A History of the Chinese in America To 1910*. Illustrated by Earl Thollander. New York: Doubleday, 1967. Incorporated into this lively, illustrated text is the story of how Yankee clipper ships brought the news of the California gold rush to China and subsequently brought back thousands of Chinese who helped build the first railway across the West. The Chinese settlement in San Francisco and a brief look at today's settlement concludes this story.
—*Chinese Americans/history/secondary*.

Chun, Shinae and Patricia Donegan. *A Passage Through the Hermit Kingdom*. Deerfield, Ill.: Asia Press, 1980. This resource book about Korea is divided into topical sections and covers ancient Korea and modern South Korea.
—*Korea/history/intermediate/secondary*.

Fawdry, Marguerite. *Chinese Childhood. A Miscellany of Mythology, Folklore, Fact and Fable*. Barron's, 1977. A veritable storehouse of information about customs and habits of the Chinese. The book had its beginnings as a catalog for Pollock's Toy Museum (London) exhibition on Chinese Childhood in 1973. The author found that the West is indebted to China for "roses and pandas; tops and diabolos, for spillikins, puppets, puzzles, kites, ..." in addition to gunpowder, silk, paper, etc.
—*China/culture/secondary/general*.

Fritz, Jean. *China Homecoming*. Photographs by Michael Fritz. New York: Putnam, 1985. A sequel to the author's *Homesick*. Born and raised in China, the author left when she was 13 and cherished fond memories of her first homeland for over 40 years. This volume describes her emotional "homecoming" in 1976 after 45 years.
—*China/culture/general/secondary*.

Gross, Susan Hill, and Marjorie Wall Bingham. *Women in India: Vedic to Modern Times*. Hudson, Wisc.: Gary E. McCuen Publications, 1980. Surveys the history, status, and roles of women in India from ancient times to the modern period. Includes selected readings and study questions. Each unit includes a set of books, a teacher's guide, and a sound filmstrip.
—*India/history/secondary*.

Gross, Susan Hill, and Marjorie Wall Bingham. *Women in Traditional China: Ancient Times to Modern Reform*. Hudson, Wisc.: Gary E. McCuen, 1980. Surveys the history, status, and roles of women in Chinese society from ancient times up to, but not including, the modern period. Includes se-

lected readings with study questions. Each unit includes a set of books, a teacher's guide, and a sound filmstrip.
—*China/history/seconday.*

Hantula, James Neil, et al. *Global Insights: People and Cultures.* (For full citation, see Intermediate Section.)

Houston, Jeanne Wakatsuki and James Houston. *Farewell to Manzanar: A True Story of Japanese American Experience During and After The World War II Internment.* Boston, Mass: Houghton-Mifflin, 1973. This recollection of a family's internment in a relocation camp in California is told through the eyes of a seven-year-old, uprooted from her home and undergoing an experience she can in no way understand. Explicit in its detail concerning everyday life in the camp, the book transcends the issue into universal human concerns.
—*Japanese Americans/literature/secondary/general.*

"India, a Teacher's Guide," in *Focus on Asian Studies;* New York: The Asia Society, 1985. Prepared for the special occasion of the "Festival of India" year 1985-86. The guide uses an interdisciplinary approach and is focused with special chapters on "Contemporary Society," "Identity," "Perception," and "Expression of Reality, Values, and Decision Making." Each chapter has a section of background readings and activities and a section of student readings, which are the key to the classroom activities. An excellent guide.
—*India/reference/culture/intermediate/secondary.*

Ishigo, Estelle. *Lone Heart Mountain.* Los Angeles, 1972. This true story of a family during the Japanese American relocation in World War II is a human, well-written account of what occurs when an established way of life changes abruptly. Copies of letters to Mrs. Ishigo from the Provost Marshall are included along with excellent illustrations. The book is moving and readable.
—*Japanese Americans/literature/secondary/general.*

Jaffrey, Madhur. *Seasons of Splendour: Tales, Myths and Legends of India.* (For full citation, see Intermediate section.)

Johnson, Donald and Jean, eds. *Through Indian Eyes.* 2 vols. New York: Center for International Training and Education, 1981. The main goal of these two volumes is to present an Indian view of India and the world. Almost all the material in these two volumes comes from Indians. These volumes do not explain India but show it.
—*India/history/secondary.*

Kim, Yong Choon. *Oriental Thought: An Introduction to the Philosophical and Religious Thought of Asia.* Totowa, N.J.: Littlefield, Adams and Co., 1973. An analytical, comparative, and critical approach to oriental thought.
—*Asia/culture/secondary/general.*

Knoll, Tricia. *Becoming Americans: Asian Sojourners, Immigrants, and Refugees in the Western United States.* Portland, Oreg: Coast to Coast Books, 1982. Written by a high school teacher, this book examines the experiences of Asians in America, beginning with the Chinese of the 1850s to the

Vietnamese of the 1980s, through historical documents, novels, poems, autobiographies, and photographs. Highly recommended.
—*Asian Americans/history/secondary.*

Lawson, Don. *The Eagle and the Dragon: The History of U.S.-China Relations.* New York: Crowell, 1985. Traces the relationship between the United States and China from the China trade in the eighteenth century to the reopening of official relations in the 1970s.
—*China/history/secondary.*

Lawson, Don. *The United States in the Vietnam War.* New York: Crowell, 1981. Begins with a brief review of the French effort to establish control in Vietnam after World War II; and ends with American involvement and withdrawal.
—*Southeast Asia/history/secondary.*

Liang, Heng and Judith Shapiro. *Son of the Revolution.* New York: Vintage Books, 1983. Describes the political events of the cultural revolution in human terms. Also the book presents a picture of Liang Heng's family torn apart by the events in China. Liang is exhilarated by participation in political events and ecstatic to catch a glimpse of Mao Zedong, but this is mixed with the pain of his own family's persecution. Liang Heng was 12-years-old when the Cultural Revolution gained momentum.
—*China/history/secondary/general.*

Loescher, Gil with Ann Dull Loescher. *China: Pushing Toward the Year 2000.* New York: Harcourt Brace & Jovanovich, 1983. Discusses events that led to the rise of the Chinese Communist party and outlines policies that many believe will modernize this developing agrarian country.
—*China/history/secondary.*

McCunn, Ruthanne Lum. *Thousand Pieces of Gold: A Biographical Novel.* San Francisco: Design Enterprises, 1981. Fictionalized biography of a Chinese girl. She was sold by her starving parents to bandits and then shipped off to America, where she struggles for her freedom.
—*Chinese Americans/literature/secondary/general.*

Minear, Richard, ed. *Through Japanese Eyes,* 2 vols. New York: Center for International Training and Education, 1981. These volumes attempt to let the Japanese speak for themselves. The readings are mostly written by Japanese. The editor does not explain Japan but shows it through the writings of Japanese people.
—*Japan/history/secondary.*

Newlon, Clarke. *China, The Rise to World Power.* New York: Dodd, Mead, 1983. Explores the history of China, emphasizing its development into a giant communist power and its importance in the contemporary world.
—*China/history/secondary.*

Oh, Sadaharu and David Falkner. *Sadaharu Oh: A Zen Way of Baseball.* New York: Times Books, 1984. Oh was Japan's greatest baseball player until his retirement in 1980 after 22 years as first baseman for the Tokyo Giants. This engrossing autobiography is not only the chronicle of a baseball player and his career, but also the powerful and moving story

of how disciplined training and the vision and guidance of an inspired teacher led a simple man to achievement and enlightenment. This autobiography reveals the Japanese emphasis on team spirit and showing politeness and respect toward opponents and their fans.
—*Japan/culture/secondary/general.*

Piggott, Juliet. *Japanese Mythology.* New York: Peter Bedrick Books, 1983. Describes many of the ghosts and animal legends of Japanese traditional religion.
—*Japan/literature/secondary.*

Rau, Margaret. *Holding Up the Sky: Young People in China.* New York: E.P. Dutton, 1983. Describes the daily lives, work, and aspirations of representative young Chinese between the ages of 18 and 29 in various parts of China. History, politics, education, health care, marriage, and occupational choices are interwoven. An excellent basis for comparative cultural study.
—*China/culture/secondary.*

Rawding, F.W. *The Rebellion in India, 1857.* New York: Cambridge University Press, 1977. An account of the establishment of the English East India Company, the growth of British power in India, and the mutiny of 1857 in which the Indian soldiers in the Bengal Army revolted against their British officers.
—*India/history/intermediate.*

Rose, Peter I. *They and We: Race and Ethnic Relations in the United States.* New York: Random House, 1964. A good introduction to race, ethnicity, and social status in America, which can be read with understanding by high school students. The author's distinction between prejudice and discrimination is especially useful.
—*Ethnic studies/general/secondary.*

Sanders, Tao Tao Liu. *Dragons, Gods and Spirits from Chinese Mythology.* Illustrated by Johnny Pau. New York: Schocken Books (World Mythology Series), 1983. Based on Chinese scholarly sources and compiled in story form, this collection attempts to show the most representative of Chinese myths and legends. Well illustrated.
—*China/literature/secondary.*

Schwartz, Rudolph, Harold Hammond, and Adriane Ruggiero. *Japan-Korea-Taiwan: History, Culture, People.* New York: Globe Book, 1981. Provides an overview of the role that thousands of years of tradition have played in shaping Japan, Korea, and Taiwan.
—*Japan/Korea/Taiwan/China/history/intermediate/secondary.*

Seybolt, Peter, ed. *Through Chinese Eyes,* 2 vols. New York: Center for International Training and Education, 1981. These two volumes let the Chinese speak for themselves. Most of the readings were written by Chinese. The goal of the author is to show rather than to explain.
—*China/history/secondary.*

Takashima, Shizuye. *A Child in Prison Camp.* Montreal: Tundra books, 1983. Following December 7, 1941, 22,000 Japanese Canadians were faced

with three years of internment. Takashima describes the outrageous injustices as they appeared to her as a young and sensitive girl. High school students will want to read this evocative book themselves. Teachers may want to read portions of it to younger children.
—*Japanese Americans/literature/secondary/general.*

Talbot, Phillips. *India in the 1980s.* New York: Foreign Policy Association, 1983. A brief introduction to India as a land of diverse cultures, contrasts, and seemingly endless contradictions. The book provides a view of India that helps balance the stereotypical image of India as an ancient unchanging land of spiritual gurus, natural disasters, and poverty.
—*India/history/secondary.*

Traub, James. *India: The Challenge of Change,* rev. ed. New York: Juian Messner, 1985. A description of modern India and its development, including chapters on daily life, religion, government, agriculture and industry, and foreign relations.
—*India/history/secondary.*

Tsuboi, Sakae. *Twenty-Four Eyes.* Translated by Akira Miura. Rutland, Vt.: Charles E. Tuttle, 1983. A deeply pacifist novel about a devoted country school teacher and her 12 students who must take part in the war. Story of innocence attempting to survive in a world of cruel priorities, corrupt values, and war-torn modern Japan. An excellent film by the same name based on the same story is also available.
—*Japan/literature/secondary/general.*

"Vietnam: A Teacher's Guide," in *Focus on Asian Studies.* New York: The Asia Society, 1983. This guide contains five chapters, which deal briefly with the recent situation in Vietnam beginning with the French presence there ending with the U.S. withdrawal. Each chapter answers the questions what, who, when, why, and where. Each chapter also has suggested classroom activities. A useful issue. Also has a resource chapter which lists books, films, and other sources.
—*Southeast Asia/History/secondary.*

Watts, William. *The United States and Asia: Changing Attitudes and Policies.* Lexington, Mass: Lexington Books, 1982. Examines Asia's place in the world, American knowledge and stereotypes of Asia, and United States-Asian relations and commitments.
—*Asia/history/secondary.*

Whitney, Clara A.N. *Clara's Diary: An American School Girl in Meiji Japan.* Edited by M. William Steele and Tamiko Ichimata. New York: Kadansha International, distributed by Harper & Row, 1981. The personal record of a 14-year-old girl who arrived in Japan in 1875, just as Japan was emerging from 250 years of isolation. An interesting record, especially inlight of the fact that Japan was at the time just beginning its modernization drive.
—*Japan/history/secondary/general.*

Wu Ch' eng-en. *Monkey: A Folk Novel.* Translated by Arthur Waley. New York: Grove Press; 1958. An abridged translation of a highly popular and

amusing novel of comic satire, *Monkey* is a folk novel of the sixteenth century about a monk named Tripitaka and his three colorful disciples on their pilgrimage to India to bring back Buddhist scriptures to China. However it is Tripitaka's disciple, the roguish Monkey and his "irreverent spirit and exuberant vitality" that dominate and give life to the story. Monkey is a unique combination of beauty with absurdity, of profundity with pure nonsense. For the full unabridged four-volume translation by Anthony Yu entitled *Journey to the West* (University of Chicago Press, 1977-85), check your local library.
—*China/literature/secondary/general.*

For General Readers

ASIA AND ASIAN AMERICANS

This section contains over 200 items. It is subdivided into five areas: Asia and Asian Americans (approximately 40 items); China and Chinese Americans (approximately 60); India and Indian Americans (approximately 30); Japan and Japanese Americans (approximately 50); and other Asian groups, which include Koreans, Filipinos, and Southeast Asians (approximately 45). Other Asian groups are placed in the last category because of the relatively small number of works as compared to China, Japan, and India.

Asian American is a term of recent coinage. It gained popular usage during the 1960s and is used to refer to a diverse group of people from countries of East Asia, Southeast Asia, South Asia, and the Pacific Islands. Because of the cultural diversity of these people it is sometimes difficult to generalize about Asian Americans as a whole. They do not function as a unified group.

The first section, however, deals with Asian Americans as a group. There are a number of reference works in this section that will point the reader toward other sources of information. The most comprehensive bibliography is *Asians in America: A Selected Annotated Bibliography* published by the Asian American Studies Program of the University of California at Davis. The most comprehensive source book on Asian Americans is Emma Gee's *Counterpoint: Perspectives on Asian America.*

All-Asia Guide, 12th ed. Rutland, Vt.: Charles E. Tuttle, 1982. An all-Asia travel guide arranged by country. Each section has background history, maps, information about passports, currency, language, climate, etc.
—*Asia/reference/general.*
Anderson, G.L. *Asian Literature in English: A Guide to Information Sources.* Detroit, Mich.: Gale Research Co., 1981. This guide, excellent for library use, is organized by country for easy reference. There are bibliographies for each country and region for further research.
—*Asia/reference/general.*
Asian American Librarians caucus, compiler. *Asian Americans: An Annotated Bibliography for Public Libraries.* Chicago: American Library Association, 1977. This annotated list of books on Asian Americans is divided into five sections dealing with Asian Americans in general, Chinese Americans, Japanese Americans, Korean Americans, and Filipino Americans.
—*Asian Americans/reference.*

Asian American Materials (Catalog). San Mateo, Calif.: Japanese American Curriculum Project, 1986-1987. The Japanese American Curriculum Project is the largest retailer of Asian American materials in the United States and has been in existence for 17 years. The store carries books, dolls, records, and magazines.
—*Asian Americans/reference.*

Asians In America: A Selected Annotated Bibliography. An Expansion and Revision. Davis, Calif.: Asian American Studies, University of California, Davis, 1983. Most comprehensive bibliography to date on Asian Americans, includes 1,529 entries. End date 1979. Subject areas: Asian Experience (230 entries), Chinese Experience (499 entries), Japanese Experience (550 entries), Filipino Experience (101 entries), Korean Experience (42 entries), East Indian Experience (53 entries). Covers historical, ecnomic, political, communal, social, psychological and educational aspects of the American experience.
—*Asian Americans/reference/general.*

Banks, James A., ed. *Teaching Ethnic Studies: Concepts and Strategies* (Yearbook). Washington, D.C.: National Council for Social Studies, 1973. An important book. A hard-hitting volume written by a group of teachers and researchers committed to social justice but not uniform in their approaches. The book will evoke strong emotions—pain, anger, sorrow, compassion, disillusionment, despair, admiration, and hope. Not a theoretical book, but one in which the authors give concrete advice that teachers can use in the classroom to combat racism and discrimination, and develop sensitivity to ethnic differences. There are chapters on Asian Americans, Blacks, Chicanos, Native Americans, and Puerto Ricans. An indispensable book, which should be on every teacher's bookshelf.
—*Ethnic studies/Asian Americans/reference/general.*

A Bibliography of Asian and Asian American Books for Elementary School Youngsters. Olympia, Wash.: Superintendent of Public Instruction, 1975. This bibliography lists books for youngsters about Asian Americans. Each work is rated on its sensitivity to racial differences, accuracy of facts, readability, and interest level. More works of this kind should be encouraged. Project was sponsored by the Asian American Cultural Heritage Program and the Asian American Education Association.
—*Asian Americans/reference/general.*

Bronner, Elizabeth H., compiler. A Storyteller's Guide to Asian Folktales. Singapore: Children's Services, National Library, 1979. Bibliography for Afghanistan, Burma, China, India, Indonesia, Iran, Japan, Korea, Malaysia, Pakistan, Philippines, Singapore, Sri Lanka, Thailand, and Vietnam. An important source because it gives much bibliographic information plus storytelling time, appropriate age group, and the nature of the story.
—*Asia/reference/literature.*

Bullard, Betty M. *Asia in New York City: A Guide.* New York: Asia Society, 1981. A quick reference for business, teachers, students, and tourists who

want information about Asian resources in metropolitan New York. Compiled by the Asia Society. Includes museums, exhibits, restaurants, book and record stores, craft shops, art galleries, movie houses, radio and television stations, consulates, and more.
—Asia/reference/general.

*Cheung, King-kok and Stan Yogi, eds. *Asian American Literature: An Annotated Bibliography.* New York: Modern Language Association, 1988. Contains some 3,400 entries on Asian American creative literary works. The annotations are brief and clear.
—Asian Americans/literature/reference.

*Chin, Frank, Jeffery Paul Chan, Lawson Fusao Inada, and Shawn Wong, eds. *Aiiieeeee! An Anthology of Asian American Writers.* New York: Doubleday Anchor Books, 1975. This volume includes the writings of 14 accomplished Americans of Japanese, Chinese, and Filipino descent. It spans the spectrum of literary genres with surrealistic prose/poetry, plays, autobiographies, short stories, and excerpts from novels. A long overdue volume. The pieces assembled here are by turns angry, wistful, belligerent, and elegiac. Reflects the concerns of the new generation of Asian Americans.
—Asian Americans/literature/general.

Chu, Bernice, ed. *The Asian American Media Reference Guide.* New York: Asian CineVision, 1986. Includes more than 550 films and video programs either produced by Asian and Asian Americans or about Asians and Asian Americans. A useful annotated bibliography. The first of its kind.
—Asian Americans/reference/general.

Civil Rights Issues of Asian and Pacific Americans: Myths and Realities. Washington, D.C.: U.S. Commission on Civil Rights, 1979. A veritable storehouse of information about all and every aspect of Asian and Pacific Americans. This volume is the full proceedings of a consultation sponsored by the U.S. Commission on Civil Rights on May 8-9, 1979. A valuable resource.
—Asian Americans/history/general.

*Daniels, Roger. *Asian American: Chinese and Japanese in the United States Since 1858.* Seattle: University of Washington Press, 1988. Daniels presents a basic history comprising the political and socioeconomic background of Chinese and Japanese immigration and acculturation, how it was similar to and how different from European immigration experiences, and illuminates the tensions within our modern multiracial society.
—Asian Americans/history/general.

Dunn, Lynn P. *Asian Americans: A Study Guide and Sourcebook.* San Francisco: R & E Research Associates, 1975. This is one of a four-volume series on American minorities. Each volume deals with the themes of identity, conflict, and integration/nationalism. Useful but somewhat dated—the author frequently uses the term "oriental" when referring to Asians.
—Asian Americans/reference/general.

Fairservis, Walter A., Jr. *Asia: Traditions and Treasures.* Color photographs by Lee Boltin. New York: Abrams, 1981. Tells the story of the continent's myriad peoples, casting light on ways of life going back to earliest times.
—*Asia/history/general.*

Focus On Asian Studies. New York: Asia Society, Inc., 1980-. An excellent source for the most recent publications on Asia, Asian Studies, and Asian American studies. Dedicated to deepening American understanding of Asia. Articles and essays are written from the pedagogical viewpoint for use by teachers in the schools. An excellent teaching aid.
—*Asia/reference/teachers.*

*Gee, Emma, et al. eds. *Counterpoint: Perspectives on Asian America.* Los Angeles: Asian American Studies Center, UCLA, 1976. This volume is a sequel to *Roots: An Asian American Reader.* Includes 54 articles and essays, 31 short stories, and over 130 illustrations. The most comprehensive anthology to date dealing with various aspects of Asians in America. Challenges the conventional approaches to the study of the Asian American experience. Divided into three parts, Part I offers bibliographical essays and book reviews, which critique the conventional approaches; Part II covers some of the present concerns of Asian Americans; Part III is devoted to the literary works of Asian American writers. Reflects the attitude of the new generation of Asian American specialists. Indispensable. Highly recommended.
—*Asian Americans/culture/general.*

Houston, James and Jeanne Wakatsukki Houston. *One Can Think About Life After the Fish is in the Canoe: And Other Coastal Sketches/Beyond Manzanar: And Other Views of Asian American Womanhood.* Santa Barbara: Capra Press, 1985. Essays on Asian American women by a Japanese American woman writer.
—*Japanese Americans/culture/general.*

Hsu, Kai-yu and Helen Palubinskas. *Asian American Authors.* Boston: Houghton Mifflin, 1972. An anthology of Asian American writings in a more conventional vein as compared to Frank Chin's *Aiiieeeee!*
—*Asian Americans/literature/general.*

Hundley, Norris, ed. *The Asian American Experience.* Santa Barbara, Calif.: Clio Books, 1976. A collection of essays on the Asian American experience.
—*Asian Americans/history/general.*

Isaacs, Harold R. *Images Of Asia: American Views Of China and India.* New York: Harper & Row, Harper Torchbooks, 1972. A combination of research and journalism, this book is an inquiry into American ideas and impressions of China and India, particularly the Chinese and Indian people. The author shows that our impressions and images of a people change with the political and social climate of the time. Although written in the 1950s, the study is still timely.
—*China/India/history/general.*

*Jenkins, Esther and Mary C. Austin. *Literature for Children About Asian and Asian Americans: Analysis and Annotated Bibliography, With Additional Readings for Adults.* New York: Greenwood Press, 1987. Addressed primarily to teachers but not exclusively, this volume is devoted to literature for young people of and about Asians and Asian Americans, including Chinese, Japanese, Koreans, and various clutural groups in Southeast Asia. Each section is prefaced with a useful introduction. Asian Indians are not included.
—*Asian Americans/reference/general.*

Kim, Elaine H. with Janice Otani. *With Silk Wings. Asian American Women at Work.* Oakland, Calif.: Asian Women United of California, 1983. Contains a number of biographical studies of outstanding Asian American women. A much needed work.
—*Asian Americans/culture/general.*

*Kim, Hyung-chan, ed. *Asian American Studies: An Annotated Bibliography and Research Guide.* New York: Greenwood Press, 1989. Contains some 3,400 entries including books, articles, and dissertations on Asian American literature in social, behavioral sciences, and humanities. Creative writing on the Asian American experience is not included. The annotations are detailed and provide useful information for the specialist and researcher.
—*Asian Americans/reference.*

Kim, Yong Choon. *Oriental Thought: An Introduction to the Philosophical and Religious Thought of Asia.*(For full citation, see Secondary Section.)

Lanansa, Philip. *A Handbook of Activities and Resources for Teaching About Asian Americans in the Elementary School.* Lexington, Mass.: Ginn Custom Publishing, 1983. Designed to provide better understanding among students belonging to non-Asian ethnic groups of the culture and heritage of their Asian American classmates.
—*Asian Americans/reference/general.*

Mangiafico, Luciano. *Contemporary American Immigrants: Patterns of Filipino, Korean and Chinese Settlement in the United States.* New York, London: Praeger, 1988. Social conditions of Asian Americans in the United States.
—*Asian Americans/history/general.*

Melendy, H. Brett. *Asians in America: Filipinos, Koreans, and East Asians.* Boston: Twayne, 1977. A general survey of the history of Asians in America focusing on the Filipinos, Koreans, and other groups.
—*Asian Americans/history/general.*

Moy, Peter. *An Annotated List of Selected Resources for Promoting and Developing an Understanding of Asian Americans.* Trenton: Reprinted by the New Jersey State Department of Education, OEEO (Originally published by the OEEO of Wisconsin, Dept. of Public Instruction), 1978. A selected list of some 140 resources on Asian Americans including books, articles, and films. A useful list.
—*Asian Americans/reference/general.*

*Poon, Wei Chi. *A Guide for Establishing Asian American Core Collections*. Berkeley: Asian American Studies Libraries, University of California, 1989. A timely much needed up-to-date guide on how to establish an Asian American library collection by one of the outstanding directors of an Asian American Studies Library.
—*Asian Americans/reference.*

"The Portrayal of Asian Americans in Children's Books." *Interracial Books for Children Bulletin*. New York: Council on Interracial Books for Children, 1976. A highly critical assessment of the portrayal, in pictures as well as text, of Asian Americans in children's and young adults' books by a new generation of Asian Americans. A much needed evaluation.
—*Asian Americans/literature/general.*

Reischauer, Edwin O., John K. Fairbank, and Albert M. Craig. *A History of East Asian Civilization*. 2 vols. Boston: Houghton Mifflin, 1960, 1962, 1965. One of the best general texts on Asian history by three authorities on East Asia at Harvard University. Countries include China, Japan, and Korea. The first volume deals with the traditional period up to the nineteenth century, the second volume covers the modern period from the nineteenth century to the present. Written in general, nontechnical language.
—*Asia/history/college.*

Shimer, Dorothy Blair, ed. *The Mentor Book of Modern Asian Literature: From the Khyber Pass to Fuji*. New York: New American Library, Mentor Book, 1969. This anthology of modern poetry, drama, fiction, and essays from 11 countries of Asia (India, China, Japan, Pakistan, Ceylon—now known as Sri Lanka—Indonesia, Nepal, Korea, Thailand, Burma, the Philippines) reflects the enormous literary vitality and diversity of the region, especially in light of the cultural metamorphoses that have taken place as age-old individual traditions have interacted with the influences of the West. Can be considered a continuation of John D. Yohannan's *A Treasury Of Asian Literature*.
—*Asia/literature/general.*

Sue, Stanley and James K. Morishima. *The Mental Health of Asian Americans*. San Francisco: Jossey-Bass, 1983. Reviews the literature on Asian American mental health and applies this research knowledge to suggest improved ways of helping members of this ethnic group.
—*Asian Americans/culture (mental health)/general.*

Tachiki, Amy, Eddie Wong, Franklin Odo, Buch Wong, eds. *Roots: An Asian American Reader*. Los Angeles: University of California, 1971. *Roots* is the basic text of the Asian American consciousness that emerged in the 1960s. It provides one of the best introductions to the Asian American experience as well as a basis for further study. Arranged under the topics of identity, history, and community, this book reflects the attitudes of the new generation of Asian Americans.
—*Asian Americans/culture/general.*

*Takaki, Ronald T. *Strangers From a Different Shore: A History of Asian Americans*. Boston: Little, Brown, 1989. The most recent and authoritative history of Asian Americans by one of the foremost Asian American scholars in the field. Takaki not only uses the standard historical sources in the field but also literature, oral histories, newspapers, magazines, and family histories.
—*Asian Americans/history/general.*

Wand, David Happell Hsin-fu, ed. *Asian American Heritage: An Anthology of Prose and Poetry*. New York: Washington Square Press, Pocket Books, 1974. A collection of prose and poetry by Asian American authors.
—*Asian Americans/literature/general.*

Wheeler, Thomas C., ed. *The Immigrant Experience. The Anguish of Becoming American*. New York: Penguin Books, 1984. Nine immigrants, all talented writers, from various parts of the world, including Asia, describe the cost and pain of becoming Americans. These nine original essays and biographies were written especially for this volume. Highly personal accounts, extraordinary self-revelation. Included are the Irish, Black, Jewish, Chinese, Polish, Norwegian, English, and Italian experience. The essays show that each must pay a price and make sacrifices to become an American, and sometimes the cost has been high.
—*Ethnic studies/history/general.*

Wong, Patricia M.Y. *Asian and Asian American Picture Books: A Selected Annotated Bibliography*. Berkeley: School of Library and Information Science, University of California, 1984. The annotations in this bibliography of children's picture books are of an evaluative nature. The books are in the collection of the Oakland Public Library's Asian Branch. The titles are examined for stereotypical and/or negative images of Asian and Asian American people, possible sexist representations, and relevance to contemporary society or historical value. The annotations are detailed.
—*Asian Americans/reference/general.*

Yohannan, John D., ed. *A Treasury of Asian Literature*. New York: New American Library, A Mentor Book, 1956. Encompassing the literatures of five countries—China, India, Arabia, Iran, and Japan—and five of the world's major religions, this volume of prose, drama, poetry, and scripture deals with widely divergent cultures, civilizations, and attitudes, and offers a valuable key for understanding the peoples of the East. Rich in entertainment and a valuable and much needed book. With introduction, individual commentaries, and bibliographies.
—*Asia/literature/general.*

CHINA AND CHINESE AMERICANS

The Chinese were the earliest and most numerous of the Asian immigrant groups to come to America. They came during the gold rush days in the 1850s, settling first in California and then gradually moving eastward. The Chinese were the first Asians to suffer prejudice and discrimination culminating in the Exclusion Act of 1882. It was not until 1943 that the Exclusion Act was repealed. Some recent titles that recount this experience are Jack Chen's *The Chinese of America*, Maxine Hong Kingston's novel *Woman Warrior*, about a Chinese American woman's search for her identity, and playwright David Henry Hwang's anthology, *Broken Promises*

Chan, Sucheng. *This Bitter-Sweet Soil: The Chinese in California Agriculture*, 1860-1910. Berkeley: University of California Press, 1987. This book focuses on the lives and work of thousands of Chinese truck gardeners, tenant farmers, commission merchants, labor contractors, farmer laborers, and farm cooks in the rural areas of California. A healthy antidote to the many studies of urban Chinatowns. Shows these early immigrants were not just laborers but agricultural pioneers and entrepreneurs. The author is Professor of History and Provost of Oakes College, University of California, Santa Cruz.
—*Chinese Americans/history/general.*
Chen, Jack. *The Chinese of America: From the Beginning to the Present.* San Francisco: Harper & Row, 1980. This solidly documented yet highly readable account of the Chinese in America highlights the part the Chinese played in founding wineries, mining gold, building railroads, and contributing to mercantile expansion. Offers a deeply moving, coherent account of anti-Chinese agitation, the tragedy of the exclusion laws, and the creation of ghetto Chinatowns—all told from a Chinese American perspective. The most recent and probably the best general account. An important work.
—*Chinese Americans/history/general.*
Chin, Frank. *The Chickencoop Chinaman/The Year of the Dragon.* Seattle: University of Washington Press, 1981. Two plays by a controversial Chinese American writer, which defy accepted stereotypes and conventions. Chin addresses the fundamental questions about Chinese American identity, manhood, and culture in the congested ghettoes of Chinatown.
—*Chinese Americans/literature/general.*
Chin, Frank. *The Chinaman Pacific & Frisco R.R. Co.: Short Stories.* Minneapolis: Coffee House Press, 1988. Contains eight short stories by the radical Chinese American author.
—*Chinese Americans/literature/general.*
China in the Classroom. Resource Catalog 1987. Washington, D.C.: US-China Peoples Friendship Association, 1987. This catalog offers educators up-to-

date curriculum aids for all ages. Contains reference sections and guides for elementary, intermediate, and secondary levels, and a wide variety of materials and activities on history, literature, religion, language, women, and others, including audiovisual aids.
—*China/reference/general.*

China Resources: A Guide for the Classroom. Stanford: SPICE, Stanford University, 1986. A new, extensive guide to resource centers offering China-related teaching materials and services. Includes chapters on selected printed resources, recent audiovisual materials, and materials on Chinese Americans. A valuable tool for libraries and teachers.
—*China/reference/general.*

Ching, Frank. *Ancestors: 900 Years in the Life of a Chinese Family.* New York: Morrow, 1988. The author's search for roots in China. Traces his genealogy back to the Song dynasty (A.D. 960-1279).
—*Chinese Americans/history/general.*

Chu, Louis. *Eat a Bowl of Tea.* Seattle: Univeristy of Washington Press, 1982. A landmark work in Chinese American literature. The novel depicts everyday life of an American Chinatown's bachelor society, an enclave of old men trapped by racist immigration laws. Also, a tale of adultery and retribution. This picture of Chinatown may seem unfamiliar and forbidding, but it is real, immediate, and authentic.
—*Chinese Americans/literature/general.*

Cotterell, Arthur. *The First Emperor of China: The Greatest Archeological Find of Our Time.* New York: Holt, Rinehart & Winston, 1981. Tells of the discovery and excavation of the tomb of the first emperor of China who reigned in the third century B.C. A very readable and beautiful volume.
—*China/history/general.*

Fairbank, John K. *China Watch.* Cambridge: Harvard University Press, 1987. This collection of essays by one of the leading authorities on China focuses on the modern period. The essays were written between 1971 and 1985.
—*China/history/general.*

Fairbank, John K. *The United States and China.* 4th ed. Cambridge: Harvard University Press, 1983. Describes the fall of the imperial system, the rise of the Communist Party, and America's evolving relationship with China.
—*China/history/general.*

Fawdry, Marguerite. *Chinese Childhood. A Miscellany of Mythology, Folklore, Fact and Fable.* (For full citation, see Secondary Section.)

Fessler, Loren W., ed. *Chinese in America: Stereotyped Past, Changing Present.* New York: Vantage Press, 1983. A history of Chinese in America. Addresses the issues of Chinatown ghettos and racial prejudice. Also has information on the Mississippi Delta Chinese in the post-reconstruction South.
—*Chinese Americans/history/general.*

Fritz, Jean. *China Homecoming*. Photographs by Michael Fritz. New York: Putnam, 1985. Describes the author's travels in China since 1976.
—*China/culture/general*

Frolic, B. Michael. *Mao's People*. Cambridge: Harvard University Press, 1981. Mao's China as viewed through the lives of 16 Chinese. A look from the inside.
—*China/history/general.*

Gentzler, J. Mason. *A Syllabus of Chinese Civilization*, 2nd ed. New York: Columbia University Press, 1972. A useful guide for anyone who needs to conduct a course or give lectures on China. A handy, well-constructed guide.
—*China/referece/general/college*

Gernet, Jacques. *A History of Chinese Civilization*. Translated from the French by J. R. Foster. Cambridge, London, New York: Cambridge University Press, 1982. One of the most authoritative and comprehensive one-volume histories of China in recent years. Jacques Gernet has succeeded in synthesizing the social, political, religious, scientific, and artistic aspects of Chinese civilization and placed it in the context of the development of world civilization. An outstanding work.
—*China/history/general.*

Hartman-Goldsmith, Joan. *Chinese Jade*. Hong Kong, New York: Oxford University Press, 1986. An introduction to the significance of jade in Chinese culture as an object of art.
—*China/culture/general.*

Hoexter, Corinne. *From Canton to California: The Epic of Chinese Immigration*. New York: Four Winds Press, 1976. This book traces the history of the Chinese in America and, in particular, the history of one man, Dr. Ng Poon Chew. As editor of the first Chinese-language newspaper in the United States, Dr. Chew became the leader and the spokesperson for Chinese Americans across the nation until his death in 1931.
—*Chinese Americans/history/general.*

Hunter, Jane. *The Gospel of Gentility: American Women Missionaries in Turn-of-the-Century China*. New Haven: Yale University Press, 1984. Based on diaries and correspondence, this narrative describes the lives of American women missionaries in China—their difficulties as well as their unexpected freedom and authority. Illustrated with photographs.
—*China/history/general.*

Hwang, David Henry. *Broken Promises: Four Plays*. New York: Avon Books, 1983. The author is one of America's upcoming, young playwrights. His plays illuminate the conflicts of Chinese Americans in their struggle to integrate vastly different cultures. The plays in this anthology include: *FOB* (fresh-off-the-boat), *The Dance and the Railroad, Family Devotions*, and *The House of Sleeping Beauties*.
—*Chinese Americans/literature/general.*

Hwang, David Henry. *The Sound of a Voice*. New York: Dramatists Play Service, 1984. A new play by Hwang, one of the most promising young playwrights on Broadway today.
—*Chinese Americans/literature/general.*

Isaacs, Harold R. *Images of Asia. American Views of China and India*. New York: Harper & Row, Harper Torchbooks, 1972. A combination of research and journalism, this book is an inquiry into American ideas and impressions of China and India, particularly the Chinese and Indian people. The author shows that our impressions and images of a people change with the political and social climate of the time. Although written in the 1950s, the study is still timely.
—*China/India/history/general.*

Johnson, Kay Ann. *Women, The Family and Peasant Revolution in China*. Chicago: University of Chicago Press, 1983. Examines the policies and changes affecting rural women under Communist leadership during the revolution and since. Argues that the party often reinforced the traditional role of women to further its predominant economic and military aims.
—*China/culture/general.*

Kingston, Maxine Hong. *China Men*. New York: Alfred A. Knopf, 1980. A hard-hitting novel about the men, fathers, sons and brothers, in Ms. Kingston's fictional and real world. This is a book about becoming American in spite of rejection and misunderstanding. A powerful work filled with horror, pain, great joy, violence, and loneliness.
—*Chinese Americans/literature/general.*

Kingston, Maxine Hong. *The Woman Warrior: Memoirs of a Girlhood Among Ghosts*. New York: Knopf, 1976. An American-born Chinese woman's attempt to come to grips with the contradictions and paradoxes in her life. Tells of the often painful experience of coming to terms with one's own cultural past and adjusting to American life. An important work for understanding the Chinese American experience. Not an easy read, but a highly significant one.
—*Chinese Americans/literature/general.*

Lai, Him Mark. *The Chinese in America* 1785-1980. San Francisco: The Chinese Culture Foundation, 1980. One of the leading authorities on Chinese Americans, Mr. Lai has written a fully illustrated volume on the history of Chinese in America.
—*Chinese Americans/history/general.*

Lao She. *Rickshaw: The Novel Lo-T'o Hsiang Tzu*. Translated by Jean M. James. Honolulu: University of Hawaii Press, 1979. One of a handful of twentieth century classic novels about modern China. Written in the 1930s by one of the most beloved modern Chinese authors. Set in Peking about 1915 and first published in 1936, the novel focuses on the life of a young rickshaw puller whose tragic fate was predetermined by the social conditions of the time. His futile struggles end in failure and tragedy.
—*China/literature/general.*

Liang, Heng and Judith Shapiro. *Son of the Revolution*. New York: Vintage Books, 1983. Describes the political events of the cultural revolution in human terms. Also the book presents a picture of Liang Heng's family, torn apart by the events in China. Liang is exhilarated by participation in political events and ecstatic to catch a glimpse of Mao Zedong, but this is mixed with the pain of his own family's persecution. Liang Heng was 12 years old when the Cultural Revolution gained momentum.
—*China/history/secondary/general.*

Lin, Alice Murong Pu. *Grandmother Had No Name*. San Francisco: China Books and Periodicals, 1988. Describes the social conditions of Chinese American women in New York.
—*Chinese Americans/history/general.*

Ling, Amy. *Chinamerican Reflections: Poems and Paintings*. Lewiston, Me.: Great Raven Press, 1984. A collection of poetry and landscape paintings by a sensitive Asian American poet. She writes, "deep emotion—joy, but more often pain—impels me to write. These poems, then, are the highs and lows of my life, while the paintings reflect the serenity to strive for."
—*Chinese Americans/literature/general.*

Lord, Bette Bao. *Spring Moon*. New York: Harper & Row, 1981. Using the story of the Chang family of Suzhou, from 1892 to the 1970s, the author has described the Chang family's "search for knowledge, inner serenity, and profits" during the tumultuous period of modern Chinese history. The story and characters serve as a reminder of an age that has nearly vanished since 1949.
—*China/literature/general.*

Lyman, Stanford M. *Chinese Americans*. New York: Random House, 1974. An authoritative sociological survey of the Chinese in the United Staes. A standard work.
—*Chinese Americans/history/culture/general.*

Mair, Victor H. *Tunhuang Popular Narratives*. New York: Cambridge University Press, 1984. A collection of annotated translations of four vernacular Chinese stories dating from the seventh to tenth centuries A.D.
—*China/literature/general.*

Mark, Diane Mei Lin and Ginger Chih. *A Place Called Chinese America*. Dubuque, Ia.: Kendall Hunt, 1982. One of the most comprehensive and best illustrated of the recent works on Chinese in America. A handy teacher's guide to go with the text is also available.
—*Chinese Americans/history/general.*

McCunn, Ruthanne Lum. *Chinese American Portraits: Personal Histories 1828-1988*. San Francisco: Chronicle Books, 1988. Contains a number of biographies of Chinese Americans, which reflect the social conditions of the time.
—*Chinese Americans/history/general.*

McCunn, Ruthanne Lum. *Thousand Pieces of Gold: A Biographical Novel*. San Francisco: Design Enterprises, 1981. Fictionalized biography of a Chi-

nese girl sold by her starving parents to bandits. She is shipped off to American, where she struggles for her freedom.
—*Chinese Americans/literature/secondary/general.*

Miyazaki, Ichisada. *China's Examination Hell: The Civil Service Examinations of Imperial China.* Translated from the Japanese by Conrad Schirokauer. New Haven: Yale University Press, 1981. A meticulously researched essay on China's examination system. In spite of the high level of scholarship, the book is very readable.
—*China/history/general.*

Reischauer, Edwin O., John K. Fairbank, and Albert M. Craig. *A History of East Asian Civilization,* 2 vols. (For full citation, see Asia and Asian Americans.)

Salzman, Mark. *Iron & Silk.* New York: Random House, Vintage Books, 1986. A candid, compassionate, humorous, and compelling account of life in China as experienced by an American fresh out of college, who taught English in China for two years and studied martial arts.
—*China/culture/general.*

Shimer, Dorothy Blair, ed. *The Mentor Book of Modern Asian Literature: From the Khyber Pass to Fuji.* (For full citation, see Asia and Asian Americans.)

Shimer, Dorothy Blair, ed. *Rice Bowl Women: Writings by and About the Women of China and Japan.* New York: New American Library (A Mentor Book), 1982. A thoughtful anthology which contains 13 stories from China and 9 stories from Japan reflecting the hopes, dreams, disappointments, suffering, and struggles of the women of China and Japan from traditional to modern times.
—*China/Japan/literature/general.*

Sive, Mary Robinson. *China: A Multimedia Guide.* New York: Neal-Schuman, 1982. Up-to-date, comprehensive survey of instructional materials in various media. Divided into sectins for elementary, intermediate, and secondary grade levels. Listings include descriptive as well as critical statements.
—*China/reference/general.*

Stross, Randall E. *The Stubborn Earth: American Agriculturalists on Chinese Soil, 1898-1937.* Berkeley: University of California Press, 1987. A history of the first major American effort to aid China in the area of agriculture. This book draws upon the writings, diaries, and letters of the participants. They conceived of their mission as a purely technical quest and were frustrated by social, political, and cultural conditions. Reflects the dilemma of American attempts to aid developing countries when good intentions are affected by limited vision and poor understanding of the developing country.
—*China/history/general.*

Teaching About China: People and Daily Life. Stanford: SPICE, Stanford University, 1982. An annotated bibliography on daily life in the People's Republic of China, in traditional China, and in Chinese American

communities. Includes units for classroom use, teacher background readings, audiovisual, and supplementary materials.
—*China/reference/general.*

Teaching About China: Cultural Expressions. Stanford: SPICE, Stanford University, 1983. An annotated bibliography with selected entries on language, art, thought, literature, music, and theater. Recommends elementary and secondary materials, accessible background readings, and provides information on units developed by various East Asian outreach centers across America.
—*China/reference/general.*

Tsao Hsueh-chin. *Dream of the Red Chamber.* Translated by Chi-chen Wang. New York: Doubleday Anchor Books, 1958. Generally regarded as China's greatest novel and a masterpiece of world literature, *Dream of the Red Chamber* is an eighteenth-century novel set in Peking. It describes life in the compounds of the great house of Chia in which five generations live together with their innumerable retainers, servants, relatives, and other hangers-on. Of central concern is the love between the boy Baoyu and his beautiful cousin Black Jade. This is a highly abridged edition but gives an overall view of the novel. There is a five-volume unabridged translation by David Hawks and John Minford published by Penguin.
—*China/literature/general.*

Wang, An. *Lessons: An Autobiography.* Reading, Mass: Addison-Wesley, 1986. The autobiography of an outstanding Chinese American, Dr. An Wang, the founder of Wang Laboratories. It tells the story of Wang's life and his company, and reveals that the secrets of his success are simplicity, moderation, balance, and community responsibility, which are based on the Confucian values taught by his Chinese grandmother.
—*Chinese Americans/history/general.*

Wu Ch'eng-en. *Monkey: A Folk Novel.* (For full citation, see Secondary Section.)

Wu, Cheng-tsu, ed. *"Chink": A Documentary History of Anti-Chinese Prejudice in America* (The Ethnic Prejudice in America Series). New York: World Publishing Co., Meridian Book, 1972. Documents the origin and development of prejudice against the Chinese, from slurs in California Governor Stanford's inaugural address to the pervasive slanders of Sax Rohmer, who created the evil Dr. Fu Manchu. An important volume, which tells the history of legal, social, verbal, and physical abuse of the Chinese in America. But also gives insight into the Chinese way in America.
—*Chinese Americans/history/general.*

Yee, Albert H. *A Search for Meaning: Essays on a Chinese American.* San Francisco: Chinese Historical Society of America, 1984. Autobiography of a Chinese American educator. A psychologist by training, the author gives much personal experience and reflects profoundly on wider ethnic issues.
—*Chinese Americans/history/general.*

Yohannan, John D., ed. *A Treasury of Asian Literature.* (For full citation, see Asia and Asian Americans.)

Yu, Connie Young. *Profiles in Excellence: Peninsular Chinese Americans.* Stanford: Stanford Area Chinese Club, 1986. Contains brief biographies of 37 outstanding Chinese Americans from San Mateo and Santa Clara counties. Their stories reflect a diversity of experience, and give a good cross-section of Chinese Americans from the Bay area. Success stories, of course, but many were from humble family backgrounds.
—*Chinese Americans/culture/general.*

Yung, Judy. *Chinese Women in America: A Pictorial History.* Seattle, San Francisco: University of Washington Press & Chinese Culture Foundation, 1987. Utilizing archival data, 274 interviews, and 135 photographs, the author has compiled a work documenting the history of Chinese American women from 1834 to the present day. Yung details the hardships suffered by the new immigrants, and the conflicts faced by Chinese American women today. Smashes the stereotypes of Chinese women as China Dolls, Suzie Wongs, and Dragon Ladies.
—*Chinese Americans/history/general.*

INDIA AND INDIAN AMERICANS

Asian Indians constitute one of the most recent groups of immigrants to come to the United States along with the Koreans and Southeast Asians. One of the newest works on Asian Indians is S. Chandrasekhar's *From India to America*, a collection of essays on various aspects of the Indian immigrant experience. The Festival of India, held during 1985-86, brought forth a number of good works on India. Among them is *Festival of India in the United States 1985-1986*, the official book of the festival. In 1985 there appeared the epic film *Gandhi*, directed by Richard Attenborough, which showed Gandhi's lifelong struggle for India's independence. The film was inspired by Louis Fischer's book *The Life of Mahatma Gandhi*. Both would be excellent teaching aids. Other countries of South Asia, Pakistan, Sri Lanka, Nepal, Bangladesh, are included under India.

Berkson, Carmel, George Michell, and Wendy Doniger O'Flaherty. *Elephanta: The Cave of Shiva*. Princeton: Princeton University Press, 1983. Three descriptive essays and 77 photographs allow the reader to explore a major monument of Indian art, the sixth-century temple cave on Elephanta Island in Bombay harbor, and its extraordinary stone sculptures.
    —*India/culture/general.*
Borthwick, Meredith. *The Changing Role of Women in Bengal, 1849-1905.* Princeton: Princeton University Press, 1984. Focusing on the English-educated class of Bengali women, the study contends that positive social gains often bring unforseen negative consequences. Many reforms merely substitute a restrictive British definition of womanhood for traditional Hindu norms.
    —*India/culture/general.*
Bronner, Elizabeth H., compiler. *A Storyteller's Guide to Asian Folktales.* (For full citation, see Asia and Asian Americans.)
Buck, William. *Mahabharata*. Berkeley: University of California Press, 1981. The longest epic, in the original Sanskrit, ever composed. Together with the *Ramayana*, it embodies the essence of the Indian cultural heritage. Buck has adapted it for the contemporary reader.
    —*India/literature/general.*
Buck, William. *Ramayana: King Rama's Way.* Berkeley: University of California Press, 1981. Together with the *Mahabharata*, the Ramayana embodies the essence of the Indian heritage. Buck has adapted it for the contemporary reader.
    —*India/literature/general.*
Chandrasekhar, Sripati, ed. *From India to America: A Brief History of Immigration; Problems of Discrimination; Admission and Assimilation.* La Jolla, Calif.: Population Review Book, 1982. A timely and much needed vol-

ume on Asian Indians in America. Contains ten articles by leading authorities on various aspects of Asian Indian life in the United States, including immigration, adjustment, economic status, and ethnic anger and pride, with a bibliographic chapter.
  —*Indian Americans/culture/general.*

Daniels, Roger. *History of Indian Immigration to the United States: An Interpretive Essay.* New York: Asia Society, 1989. Originally presented to the conference on "India in America: The Immigrant Experience" in 1986 as part of the Festival in India program in 1985-86, this work traces the patterns of immigration from India to the United States over the better part of a century and relates this to the larger patterns of Asian and American migration.
  —*Indian Americans/history/general.*

Festival of India in the United States 1985-1986. New York: Harry N. Abrams, 1985. This is the official book of the Festival of India. It presents choice selections of illustrations and text from exhibitions organized by more than 35 museums. With 223 illustrations (204 in color), the book is a visual delight.
  —*India/history/general.*

Fischer, Louis. *The Life of Mahatma Gandhi.* New York: Harper & Row, 1983. The book Richard Attenborough read in 1962, which inspired him to devote himself to making a film of Gandhi's life.
  —*India/history/general.*

Gibson, Margaret A. *Accommodation Without Assimilation: Sikh Immigrants in an American High School.* Ithaca: Cornell University Press, 1988. Interesting case studies of Sikh high school students' problems in cultural assimilation.
  —*Indian Americans/general.*

Green, Martin. *Tolstoy and Gandhi: Men of Peace.* New York: Basic Books, 1983. Tolstoy, the Russian aristocrat and novelist, and Gandhi were two outwardly dissimilar figures. Yet they were, in their time, the only men to renounce the West's warlike imperialism with real authority. So argues the author in this dual biography, which shows how the themes of these two lives gradually converge despite their disparate orgins.
  —*India/history/general.*

Isaacs, Harold R. *Images of Asia: American Views of China and India.* New York: Harper & Row, Harper Torchbooks, 1972. A combination of research and journalism, this book is an inquiry into American ideas and impressions of China and India, particularly the Chinese and Indian people. The author shows that our impressions and images of a people change with the political and social climate of the time. Although written in the 1950s, the study is still timely.
  —*China/India/history/general.*

Kumar, Shiv. *Nude Before God.* New York: Vanguard, 1983. A novel about Hindu painter Ram Krishna, by a Pakistani poet/short-story writer, is an uncanny adult fairytale.
  —*India/literature/general.*

Kurian, George and Ram P. Srivastava, eds. *Overseas Indians: A Study in Adaptation.* New Delhi: Vikas Publishers (distributed by South Asia Books, Columbia, Mo.), 1983. Fifteen essays on South Asian immigrants to the United States, Canada, and other Western countries.
   —*Indian Americans/culture/general.*

Malik, Yogendra K. and Dhirendra K. Vajpeyi, eds. *India: The Years of Indira Gandhi.* Leiden, New York: E.J. Brill, 1988. Presents modern Indian history from 1947 to the present from the perspective of sociology and social anthropology.
   —*India/history/general.*

Malik, Yogendra K., ed. *South Asian Intellectuals and Social Change: A Study of the Role of Vernacular-Speaking Intellegentsia.* Columbia, Mo.: South Asian Books, 1982. A study of the intellectuals who speak their native languages, looking especially at the way they integrate traditional and modern value systems, the relationship between Westernized English-speaking elites and the masses, and the interplay of "high" culture with popular culture. The contributors to this collection trace the historic origins of these intellectuals, their transformations from sacred to secular roles, and the variety of roles they play in contemporary society.
   —*India/culture/general.*

Mukherjee, Bharati. *Darkness.* New York: Penguin Books, 1985. A powerful collection of stories exploring the complicated tensions of the immigrant experience. Mukherjee's stories of contemporary Indian immigrants painfully recreating their lives and selves in North America are brilliant.
   —*Indian Americans/literature/general.*

Proctor, Raja. *Waiting for Surabiel.* Queensland: University of Queensland Press, 1981. This story by a modern writer from Sri Lanka has significance for almost every third world nation that acquired independence this century. Describes the changes that Surabiel experiences as the forces of independence touch him.
   —*India/literature/general.*

Rao, V.V. Prakasa and V. Nandini Rao. *Marriage, the Family and Women in India.* Columbia, Mo.: South Asia Books, 1982. A series of essays that examines change in the Indian family structure over the past 30 years. Topics include: arranged marriage, the status of women, and employed and unemployed mothers.
   —*India/culture/general.*

Rudolph, Susanne Hoeber and Lloyd I. Rudolph. *Gandhi: The Traditional Roots of Charisma.* Chicago: University of Chicago Press, 1983. In this scholarly work two political scientists examine the way in which Gandhi was able to revitalize tradition while simultaneously breaking with some of India's entrenched values, practices, and interests.
   —*India/history/general.*

Rushdie, Salman. *Midnight's Children.* New York: Alfred A. Knopf, 1981. A modern novel about India detailing the author's experiences growing up in Bombay between 1947 and 1977. The title refers to the 1,001 chil-

dren born during the first hour of India's independence. This novel is as important to India as Gunter Grass's *The Tin Drum* is to modern Germany. An outstanding and important work.
—*India/literature/general.*

Saran, Parmatma. *The Asian Indian Experience in the United States.* Cambridge, Mass.: Schenkman Books, 1985. Analyzes the life styles and patterns of adaptation of Asian Indians who immigrated to the United States since the mid-1960s. Saran, a sociologist, does a longitudinal case study of ten Indian families in the New York metropolitan area. His results suggest that the immigrants subscribe to the norms of the society for their work and professions, but maintain traditional family and friendship patterns.
—*Indian Americans/culture/general.*

Saran, Parmatma and Edwin Eames, eds. *The New Ethnics: Asian Indians in the United States.* New York: Praegar, 1980. A collection of essays on the Indian experience in the United States.
—*Indian American/culture/general.*

Shah, Giri Raj. *Indian Heritage.* New Delhi: Abhinav Publications/distributed by Humanities Press, Atlantic Highlands, N.J., 1983. Presents Indian culture and civilization through the fine arts, literature, religion, and philosophy.
—*India/history/general.*

Shimer, Dorothy Blair, ed. *The Mentor Book of Modern Asian Literature: From the Khyber Pass to Fuji.* (For full citation, see Asia and Asian Americans.)

Talbot, Phillips. *India in the 1980's.* New York: Foreign Policy Association, 1983. A brief introductin to India as a land of diverse cultures, contrasts, and seemingly endless contradictions. The book provides a view of India that helps balance the stereotypical image of India: an ancient unchanging land of spiritual gurus, natural disasters, and poverty.
—*India/history/secondary/general.*

Wolpert, Stanley. *A New History of India,* 2nd ed. New York: Oxford University Press, 1982. "The best textbook on Indian history."—Journal of Asian Studies.
—*India/history/general.*

Yohannan, John D., ed. *A Treasury of Asian Literature.* (For full citation, see Asia and Asian Americans.)

JAPAN AND JAPANESE AMERICANS

Japan and Japanese culture have attracted much attention in recent years because of Japan's economic and industrial growth. The interest, however, has not focused just on why Japan is so successful economically, but also on her culture, society, education, and history. There is interest in the status of Japanese women, the adoption of Western values in Japanese society, and the Japanese educational system.

Some books worthy of note are Sadaharu Oh's *Sadaharu Oh: A Zen Way of Baseball* on the cultural differences between baseball in the United States and Japan; Haru Matsukata Reischauer's account of her family and their relations with the United States in *Samurai and Silk*; and Sharon Sievers' *Flowers in Salt: The Beginnings of Feminist Consciousness in Modern Japan* on the feminist movement in Japan.

Aoki, Michiko Y. and Margaret B. Dardess, eds.. *As the Japanese See It: Past and Present*. Honolulu: University Press of Hawaii, 1981. The authors brought together a wealth of Japanese primary sources on the lives and values of ordinary people in their own words. Fills a major gap in materials available for the study of Japan in undergraduate survey courses on Asia. The 31 selections have been organized under four headings: 1) religion, 2) the family, 3) the community, and 4) the state. A useful general source book.
—*Japan/culture/general.*

Armor, John and Peter Write. *Manzanar = (Ringoen)*. New York: Times Books, 1988. Manzanar war relocation center, evacuation and relocation, pictorial works. Includes an essay "A mistake of terrifically horrible proportions" by John Hersey.
—*Japanese Americans/history/general.*

Bernstein, Gail Lee. *Haruko's World: A Japanese Farm Woman and Her Community*. Stanford: Stanford University Press, 1983. A readable and enjoyable book on rural Japanese women as seen through the life of a farm woman, Haruko. It describes the relationships between family and community, family and school, and the effects of mechanization of agriculture on the family. May be read in conjunction with John Nathan's film *Farm Song*.
—*Japan/culture/secondary/general.*

Bronner, Elizabeth H. *A Storyteller's Guide to Asian Folktales*. (For full citation, see Asia and Asian Americans.)

Cogan, John J. and Donald O. Schneider, eds. *Perspectives On Japan: A Guide For Teachers*. Washington, D.C.: Bulletin No. 69 of the National Council for Social Studies, 1983. Gives "classroom teachers several perspectives on Japan and the Japanese, as well as some ideas and resources for teaching these perspectives." Bulletin is divided into three parts. Part I

presents "Japan from a Japanese Perspective." Part II presents "Japan
from an Outsider's Perspective." Part III presents "Activities and Resources for Teaching about Japan." Schneider lists a number of excellent
activities on both the elementary and secondary levels for teaching
about various aspects of Japanese culture.
—*Japan/reference/general/teachers.*

Condon, Jane. *A Half Step Behind: Japanese Women of the '80s.* New York: Dodd,
Mead, 1986. A unique book on present-day Japan from the women's
point of view. Japanese women of all ages and circumstances speak out
with remarkable candor about marriage, work, family, education, di-
vorce, and widowhood. These interviews reveal that women in Japan
are changing. Women are Japan's hidden asset.
—*Japan/culture/general.*

Conrat, Richard and Maisie. *Executive Order 9066: The Internment of 110,000 Japanese Americans.* Cambridge, Mass.: M.I.T. Press, 1972. Composed of photographs, newspaper clippings, and quotes, this book covers the
internment of Japanese Americans during World War II. It presents a
devastating montage of the Japanese evacuation and white American
prejudice and hostility.
—*Japanese Americans/history/general.*

Daniels, Roger. *The Politics of Prejudice: The Anti-Japanese Movement in California
and the Struggle for Japanese Exclusion.* Berkeley, Calif.: University of California Press, 1977. This scholarly work by an outstanding historian covers the development of the anti-Japanese movement in California from
its inception in the late nineteenth century to the passage of the Immigration Act of 1924 excluding the Japanese from entering the United
States. The author shows that racism was not confined to the West or the
South, but was national in scope.
—*Japanese Americans/history/general.*

Fields, George. *From Bonsai to Levi's: When West Meets East: An Insider's Surpris-
ing Account of How the Japanese Live.* New York: Macmillan, 1984. Discusses marketing and market research in contemporary Japan.
—*Japan/culture/general.*

Fister, Pat. *Japanese Women Artists 1600-1900.* Lawrence, Kans.: Spencer Museum of Art, University of Kansas, 1988. Catalog of an exhibition of
women artists of Japan held at Spencer Museum of Art from April 2-
Mary 22, 1988.
—*Japan/culture/general.*

Hosokawa, William K. *Nisei: The Quiet Americans.* New York: William Morrow,
1969. Offers a detailed, complete look at the adversity, challenges, and
triumphs of Japanese Americans. A popular personalized narrative
about the leaders and activities of the Japanese American Citizens
League, the national organization of second generation Japanese Americans. It provides insights into the broader significance of ethnic heritage
and problems our nation faces in providing equality and justice for all.
—*Japanese Americans/history/secondary/general.*

Houston, James and Jeanne Wakatsuki Houston. *One Can Think About Life After the Fish is in the Canoe: And Other Coastal Sketches/Beyond Manzanar: And Other Views of Asian American Womanhood.* Santa Barbara, Calif.: Capra Press, 1985. Essays on Asian American women by a Japanese American woman writer.
　　—*Japanese Americans/culture/general.*
Houston, Jeanne Wakatsuki and James Houston. *Farewell to Manzanar.* (For full citation, see Secondary Section.)
Ishigo, Estelle. *Lone Heart Mountain.* (For full citation, see Secondary Section.)
Ishimoto, Baroness Shidzue. *Facing Two Ways: The Story of My Life.* Stanford, Calif.: Stanford University Press, 1984. The story of Baroness Ishimoto, who rejected the comfortable life-style of her aristocratic class when she became aware of the appalling living conditions of many Japanese women. Her work led her to become one of Japan's leading feminists.
　　—*Japan/culture/general.*
Japanese American Anthology Committee. *Ayumi: A Japanese American Anthology.* San Francisco: Japanese American Anthology Committee, 1980. A collection of fiction and poetry by Japanese American writers.
　　—*Japanese Americans/literature/general.*
Kadohata, Cynthia. *The Floating World.* New York: Viking, 1989. A confessional novel written from the point of view of a teenage girl about a Japanese immigrant family as they traverse America in the 1950s looking for work.
　　—*Japanese Americans/literature/general.*
Katai, Tayama. *Country Teacher.* Translated by Kenneth Henshall. Honolulu: University of Hawaii Press, 1984. Story is based on the diaries of a young man attempting to make his way in the adult world. Describes his compromises, disappointments, suffering, the ironic fate that cuts him down as he is on verge of finding happiness. The popularity of this 1909 novel continues to this day in Japan because of its simple depiction of the life of a common man—a young schoolteacher named Kobayashi.
　　—*Japan/literature/general.*
Katai, Tayama. *The Quilt and Other Stories.* Translated by Kenneth G. Henshall. Tokyo: University of Tokyo Press (distributed by Columbia University Press), 1981. Eight representative stories by a naturalist writer, who championed the individual and criticized the restrictive conventions of Japanese life.
　　—*Japan/literature/general.*
Kawabata, Yasunari. *Beauty and Sadness.* Translated by Howard Hibbett. New York: G.P. Putnam's Sons, 1981. This novel is Nobel Prize winner Kawabata's last novel about passion and revenge. Highly erotic and yet placid on the surface, this story of a triangular love relationship is a testament to the author's psychological mastery. A novel of supreme beauty and elegance.
　　—*Japan/literature/general.*

Kitagawa, Daisuke. *Issei and Nisei: The Internment Years:* Seabury Press, 1974. The author of this book writes vivid, first-hand descriptions of life for the Japanese American in an internment camp during World War II. He incorporates his experiences with the experiences of Japanese Americans as a whole. The book brings into focus the many differences between the Issei (first-generation) and the Nisei (second-generation) Japanese Americans within the internment camps. He also describes the way the internee saw America while in the camps. This is an important book for examining this part of American history and for getting a feeling for the Japanese American sentiment on this issue.
—*Japanese Americans/history/general.*

Lebra, Takie Sugiyama. *Japanese Women: Constraint and Fulfillment.* Honolulu: University of Hawaii Press, 1984. Studies Japanese women in Japanese society, but also contributes to cross-cultural understanding of sex roles, women's issues, socialization, aging, life cycle, and family dynamics.
—*Japan/culture/general.*

Lee, O-Young. *Smaller is Better.* New York: Kodansha International (distributed by Harper & Row, New York), 1984. Uses the "reductionist" tendency to explore such topics as why Japan modernized so easily compared to China and Korea, why the Japanese are more likely to litter a mountain trail than a city street, and why the Japanese like TV so much.
—*Japan/culture/general.*

Lippit, Noriko Mizuta and Kyoko Iriye Selden, trans. and eds. *Stories by Contemporary Japanese Women Writers.* Armonk: E.M Sharpe, 1982. Contains 12 stories by contemporary Japanese women writers.
—*Japan/literature/general.*

Makino, Yasuko. *Japan Through Children's Literature: A Critical Bibliography.* Durham, N.C.: Duke University Center for International Studies, 1978. A listing of over 150 titles carefully selected to give an accurate image and understanding of Japan and Japanese culture. Prepared with grade school children in mind. The bibliography is divided into sections on art, music, fiction, folklore and legend, poetry, and social studies.
—*Japan/reference/general.*

Masaoka, Mike M. with Bill Hosokawa. *They Call Me Moses Masaoka: An American Saga.* New York: Morrow, 1987. Biographical sketch of Mike Masaoka, a well-known Japanese American who has been involved in the Japanese American Citizens League.
—*Japanese Americans/history/general.*

Massy, Patricia. *Sketches of Japanese Crafts and the People Who Make Them.* Tokyo: Japan Times, 1980. Contents of the book cover the length and breadth of Japan and range from brushes and sumie ink to sea chests, tea whisks, paper umbrellas, charms in the shape of dogs, and kites. Massy, a practicing artist, wants to explore the "simpler beauty of inexpensive folk crafts made for generations by anonymous artisans" rather than the exclusive crafts of famous Japanese artists.
—*Japan/culture/general.*

Murakami, Hyoe with Eiji Hazumi, Kazuo Ito, James W. Heisig. *Japanese Culture in America: An Investigation into Methods of its Dissemination.* Tokyo: Japan Culture Institute, 1982. An abbreviated English-language version of a longer report published in 1981. An interesting and useful study presenting many facts and opinions about American understanding of and interest in Japan. It covers formal, academic sources, informal, festival-type occasions, and institutionalized artistic exhibits.
—*Japan/reference/general.*

Murasaki, Shikibu. *The Tale Of Genji.* Translated by Edward Seidensticker. New York: Alfred A. Knopf, 1981. Generally recognized as the greatest Japanese prose narrative and a masterpiece of world literature, this novel was written in the eleventh century by a lady in the Heian Court, Lady Murasaki. This work may be the earliest novel in the world. This complete, unabridged translation tells about the life and many love affairs of a handsome nobleman known as Prince Genji. This masterful translation is by one of the veteran translators in the field.
—*Japan/literature/general.*

Nakano, Eisha, with Barbara B. Stephen. *Japanese Stencil Dyeing: Paste-Resist Techniques.* New York: John Weatherhill, 1982. The authors give step-by-step instructions, using a variety of traditional materials and modern substitutes. Photos are included. Appendices include a list of worldwide suppliers of materials and many traditional Japanese stencil patterns.
—*Japan/culture/general.*

Ogawa, Dennis. *From Japs to Japanese.* Berkeley, Calif.: McCutchan, 1971. Examples, analogies, and quotations are used to describe the evolution of Japanese Amerian stereotypes. It traces the Japanese American stereotype from having originally been represented by negative images to now being colored with complimentary depictions.
—*Japanese Americans/history/general.*

Oh, Sadaharu and David Falkner. *Sadaharu Oh: A Zen Way of Baseball.* (For full citation, see Secondary Section.)

Reischauer, Edwin O., John K. Fairbank, and Albert M. Craig. *A History of East Asia Civilization,* 2 vols. (For full citation, see Asia and Asian Americans.)

Reishauer, Haru Matsukata. *Samurai and Silk: A Japanese and American Heritage.* Cambridge, Mass.: Belknap Press, 1986. A penetrating book on Japanese character and the forging of modern Japan. The author writes of her two illustrious grandfathers: Prince Matsukata, a provincial samurai who became one of the founding fathers of the Meiji government, and Mr. Arai, the scion of a wealthy and enterprising peasant family who almost single-handedly developed the silk trade with America.
—*Japan/Japanese Americans/history/general.*

Robins-Mowry, Dorothy. *The Hidden Sun: Women of Modern Japan.* Boulder, Colo.: Westview Press, 1983. Studies the changes in the whole of Japanese society since the war—changes in which women have been catalysts, not bystanders. With a foreword by Edwin O. Reischauer, former U.S. ambassador to Japan and Japan scholar.
—*Japan/culture/general.*

Rohlen, Thomas P. *Japan's High Schools*. Berkeley: University of California Press, 1983. This study of Japanese high schools concludes that the Japanese approach to secondary schooling is accomplished at significant human and cultural costs. Claims that a narrowness of the learning process and impoverishment of spirit accompany an efficient and effective system of mass education—one that is, in fact, unsurpassed.
—*Japan/cultural/general*.

Saint-Gilles, Amaury. *Mingei. Japan's Enduring Folk Arts*. Union City, Calif.: Heian International, 1985. This book describes many useful and decorative folk art items, serves as a source for those interested in Japanese art and culture, and form and function.
—*Japan/culture/general*.

Sakiya, Tatesuo. *Honda Motor: The Men, the Management, the Machines*. New York: Kodansha International/distributed by Harper & Row, 1983. An excellent inside look at the growth of a Japanese corporation against a backdrop of historical change. Beginning with the Meiji Restoration and continuing through World War II, the Allied Occupation and the postwar period. Not only delineates the changing fortunes of the Honda Company but also Japan's economic policies and growth.
—*Japan/history/general*.

Shimer, Dorothy Blair, ed. *The Mentor Book of Modern Asian Literature: From the Khyber Pass to Fuji*. (For full citation, see Asia and Asian Americans.)

Shimer, Dorothy Blair, ed. *Rice Bowl Women: Writings by and About the Women of China and Japan*. (For full citation, see China and Chinese Americans.)

Sievers, Sharon L. *Flowers in Salt: The Beginnings of Feminist Consciousness in Modern Japan*. Stanford: Stanford University Press, 1983. Examines the changing roles of women in Japan during the four decades following the Meiji Restoration of 1868. Concentrates on those Japanese women who were outspoken critics of their society; also assesses the contributions of women made to Japan during a period of rapid modernization.
—*Japan/culture/general*.

Stevenson, John. *Yoshitoshi's Thirty-Six Ghosts*. New York: John Weatherhill, 1983. Yoshitoshi Tsukioka, a late nineteenth-century wookblock artist, was the most highly paid woodblock designer in Japan's history. These 36 prints illustrate Japanese tales that fascinated Yoshitoshi—from charming folk stories to bloody sagas of revenge.
—*Japan/culture/general*.

Takashima, Shizuye. *A Child In Prison Camp*. (For full citation, see Secondary Section.)

Takeo, Kuwabara. *Japan and Western Civilization: Essays on Comparative Culture*. Translated by Kano Tsutomu and Patricia Murray. Tokyo: University of Tokyo Press (distributed by Columbia University Press, New York), 1984. Addresses the issue of modernization, touching on a variety of topics—both cultural and historical—from Meiji to contemporary Japan.
—*Japan/history/general*.

Tsuboi, Sakae. *Twenty-Four Eyes*. Translated by Akira Miura. (For full citation, see Secondary Section.)

Umesao, Tadao, ed. *Seventy-Seven Keys to the Civilization Of Japan*. Union City, Calif.: Heian International, 1986. Contemporary Japanese society is a mixture of old and new, traditional and technological, and native and foreign life styles. This book offers 77 keys to understanding the ways of modern Japan.
—*Japan/culture/general*.

Whitney, Clara A. N. *Clara's Diary: An American School Girl in Meiji Japan*. Edited by M. William Steele and Tamiko Ichimata. (For full citation, see Secondary Section.)

Wilson, Robert A. and Bill Hosokawa. *East to America.: A History of the Japanese in the United States*. New York: William Morrow, 1980. A "scholarly—lively—history of Japanese Americans." A collaborative project between an American scholar in history and an American-born Japanese with extensive experience in journalism. Compelling black-and-white photographs illustrate some of the finer and not so fine hours of Japanese in America.
—*Japanese Americans/history/general*.

Yohannan, John D., ed. *A Treasury of Asian Literature*. (For full citation, see Asia and Asian Americans.)

Yoshikawa, Eiji. *Musashi: An Epic Novel of the Samurai Era*. New York: Harper & Row, 1981. An authentic *Shogun*.
—*Japan/literature/general*.

OTHER ASIAN GROUPS

In recent years Koreans have become highly visable because of their various contributions to American life, from the corner grocery stores in New York City to musicians on the concert stage. Their prominence has led to a number of studies of Korean Americans. Among them is Illsoo Kim's *New Urban Immigrant: The Korean Community in New York*.

The Filipinos have played a unique role in American life because of their initial colonial status vis-a-vis the United States. Many came to the United States as low wage earners and became the object of prejudice and discrimination. Out of this experience have come moving accounts of their immigrant life, such as Carlos Bulosan's autobiography *America Is in the Heart*, which expresses his hopes, expectations, and disappointments.

The most recent group of Asian immigrants to this country are the Southeast Asians mainly from Vietnam, but also from Laos and Cambodia. For a good introduction to the complex history and culture of this region, see Milton Osborne's *Southeast Asia: An Introductory History*. There are also numerous studies of the refugee problem, including Barry Wain's *The Refused: The Agony of the Indochina Refugees*.

KOREA AND KOREAN AMERICANS

Choy, Bong-youn. *Koreans in America*. Chicago: Nelson-Hall, 1979. The author presents the socio-economic, cultural, and political activities of Koreans in America from 1882-1976, together with a history of Korea's domestic and external conditions during the same period. Choy is also a historian of Korea. An authoritative book on Korean Americans, modern Korea, and Korean American relations.
— *Korean Americans/history/general*.

Choy, Bong-youn. *Korea: A History*. Rutland, Vt.: Tuttle, 1971. An authoritative geneal cultural history of Korea from ancient times to the present.
— *Korea/history/general*.

Chung, Chong-wha, ed. *Meetings and Farewells*. Queensland, Australia: University of Queensland Press (distributed by St. Martin's Press, New York), 1980. "A collection of contemporary Korean short stories in English translation that can be recommended without reservation"—David R. Mccann.
— *Korea/literature/general*.

Chung, Chong-wha, ed. *Modern Korean Short Stories*. Kowloon, Hong Kong: Heinemann Educational Books, 1980. A collection of 12 short stories by modern Korean writers.
Korea/literature/general.

Chung, Chong-wha, trans. *Love in Mid-Winter Night: Sijo Poetry*. London, Boston: KPI, distributed by Routledge & Kegan Paul, 1985. A collection of short, lyric poetry by Korean poets.
—*Korea/literature/general*.

Kang, Younghill (1903-1972). *The Grass Roof/The Yalu Flows*. New York: Norton, 1975. Introduces American readers to the world of Korean childhood and adolescence by relating his experiences as a boy growing up in Korea. The work was first published in 1931. Also in this volume is Mirok Li's *The Yalu Flows*, originally published in 1946. Kang was professor of literature at New York University in the 1930s.
—*Korea/literature/general*.

Kendall, Laurel and Mark Peterson, eds. *Korean Women: View From the Inner Room*. New Haven: East Rock Press, 1984. A collection of essays by social historians and anthropologists that examines the much neglected topic of Korean women. These essays offer a new perspective on the workings of Korean society.
—*Korea/culture/general*.

Kim, H. Edward. *Facts About Korea*. Union City, Calif.: Heian International, 1986. Provides valuable information on the history, people, culture, customs, economy, sports, and other apsects of Korea . . . just about everything you wanted to know about Korea.
—*Korea/history/general*.

Kim, Hyung-chan and Wayne Patterson, eds. *The Koreans in America, 1882-1974: A Chronology and Fact Book*. Dobbs Ferry, N.Y.: Oceana Publications, 1974. An authoritative historical record of U.S.-Korean relations by a distinguished Korean American historian and sociologist. Lists historical dates and events, also contains documents.
—*Korean Americans/history/general*.

Kim, Hyung-chan, ed. *The Korean Diaspora: Historical and Sociological Studies of Korean Immigration and Assimilation in North America*. Santa Barbara, Calif.: ABC-Clio, 1977. An authoritative, scholarly study of the assimilation of Koreans in the United States.
—*Korean Americans/history/culture/general*.

Kim, Illsoo. *New Urban Immigrant: The Korean Community in New York*. Princeton: Princeton University Press, 1981. A sociological study of the creation and growth of the Korean community in the New York metropolitan area since 1965.
—*Korean Americans/culture/general*.

Kim, Richard E. *The Innocent*. Boston: Houghton Mifflin, 1968. A novel by a modern Korean American writer.
—*Korean Americans/literature/general*.

Kim, Richard E. *Lost Names: Scenes from a Korean Boyhood*. New York: Praeger, 1970. An autobiographical account of the author's childhood.
—*Korean Americans/literature/general*.

Kim, Richard E. *The Martyred, a Novel*. New York: G. Braziller, 1964. Novel by a Korean American writer.
—*Korean Americans/literature/general*.

Reischauer, Edwin O., John K. Fairbank, and Albert M. Craig. *A History of East Asian Civilization*. (For full citation, see Asia and Asian Americans.)

Shimer, Doroth Blair, ed. *The Mentor Book of Modern Asian Literature: From the Khyber Pass to Fuji*. (For full citation, see Asia and Asian Americans.)

Yu, Eui-young and Earl H. Phillips. *Korean Women in Transition: At Home and Abroad*. Los Angeles: Center for Korean American and Korean Studies, California State University, 1987. Describes the social conditions and employment situation of Korean women.
—*Korea/culture/general*.

THE PHILIPPINES AND FILIPINO AMERICANS

Agoncillo, Teodoro A. *A Short History of the Philippines*. New York: New American Library, Mentor Book, 1969. A general history of the Philippines from early times to the Republic by one of the leading historians on the Philippines.
—*Philippines/history/general*.

Aruego, Jose. *Juan and the Asuangs*. New York: Charles Scribner, 1970. Story of Juan and his adventures with the *asuangs*, or ghosts and spirits, of the Philippines. It tells how Juan outsmarts the *asuangs* and becomes a hero. Also provides description of other Philippine ghosts and spirits.
—*Philippines/literature/primary*.

Asian American Studies Center. *Letters in Exile: An Introductory Reader on the History of Filipinos in America*. Los Angeles: University of California, Los Angeles, 1976. An anthology of readings, including both historical and literary sources, on the Filipino experience in the United States.
—*Filipino Americans/history/general*.

Bocca, Geoffrey. *The Philippines: America's Forgotten Friend*. New York: Parents' Magazine, 1974. A history of the Philippines stressisng its political development and its tragic struggle in World War II.
—*Philippines/history/intermediate*.

Buaken, Manuel. *I Have Lived with the American People*. Caldwell, Idaho: Caxton Printers, 1948. One of the famous autobiographical accounts of Filipinos in America. Provides background information on the anti-Filipino movement in California.
—*Filipino Americans/history/general*.

Bulosan, Carlos. *America is in the Heart: A Personal History*. (For a full citation, see Secondary Section.)

Maring, Ester G. and Joel M. Maring. *Historical and Cultural Dictionary of the Philippines*. Metuchen: Scarecrow Press, 1973. A handy source, which contains approximately 1,800 entries pertaining to Filipino history, culture, physical geography, natural history, with the primary focus on history and culture.
—*Philippines/reference*.

Pido, Antonio J. A. *The Filipinos in America: Macro/Micro Dimensions of Immigration and Integration*. Staten Island, N.Y.: Center for Migration Studies, 1986. Details the growth of the Filipino diaspora, examining a variety of questions: who the Filipinos were before they migrated to the United States, why they migated, and how they relate to Americans and Americans to them once in the United States. Useful for students, scholars, immigration policy planners, and the general public.
—*Filipino Americans/history/general.*

Quinsaat, Jesse. *Letters in Exile: A Reader in the History of Filipinos in America*. Los Angeles: Asian American Studies Center, University of California at Los Angeles, 1976. A volume on the history of Filipinos in America written from the Filipino perspective. Much material here not available in standard texts and books.
—*Filipino Americans/history/general.*

Robertson, Dorothy Lewis. *Fairy Tales from the Philippines*. New York: Dodd, Mead and Co., 1971. A collection of traditional fairy tale characters and some less familiar ones, such as the *tiyanak*, or monster. These fairy tales have a lot in common with those of other languages but also present differences that make them unique. They have unusual settings and personalities providing the readers with an insight into the customs and beliefs of the people.
—*Philippines/literature/primary.*

Santos, Bienvenido N. *Scent of Apples: A Collection of Stories*. Seattle, Wash.: University of Washington Press, 1979. This collection of 16 stories portrays the lives of Filipinos in America.
—*Filipino Americans/literature/general.*

Stanley, Peter W., ed. *Reappraising an Empire: New Perspectives on Philippine-American History*. Boston: Harvard University Press, 1984. Contains 11 essays on various aspects of Philippine-American relations. The latest approaches and utilization of new materials in the National Archives of the Philippines. Topics covered include: 1) from conquest to collaboration, 2) cultural interactions, 3) economics and aspirations, and 4) independence or neo-colonialism.
—*Philippines/history/general.*

SOUTHEAST ASIA AND SOUTHEAST ASIAN AMERICANS

Farber, Don. *Taking Refuge in L.A.: Life in a Vietnamese Buddhist Temple*. New York: Aperture Foundation, 1978. Tells of the religious life of Vietnamese Americans in Los Angeles with pictures and words.
—*Vietnamese Americans/social history/general.*

Freeman, James M. *Hearts of Sorrow: Vietnamese American Lives*. Stanford, Calif.: Stanford University Press, 1989. Details the lives of Vietnamese refugees in the United States.
—*Vietnamese Americans/history/general.*

Hendricks, Glenn, Bruce T. Downing, Amos Deinard, eds. *The Hmong in Transition*. Staten Island, NY: Center for Migration Studies, 1986. Presented by 30 leading experts in the field, this volume addresses the effects of mass migration on the Hmong in France, Australia, Thailand, and the United States. Provides background information about and insights into Hmong social structure, culture, and character, commentaries on their marginality in China, their original homeland, and in Loas, assessment of their present situation in Southeast Asia and in the United States.
—*Southeast Asian Americans/history/culture/general.*

Hensler, Paul G. with Jeanne Wakatsuki Houston. *Don't Cry, It's Only Thunder.* Garden City: Doubleday, 1984. Describes the experiences of the author in working with Vietnamese children in orphanages.
—*Southeast Asia/history/general.*

Kelly, Gail P. *From Vietnam to America: A Chronicle of Vietnamese Immigration to the United States.* Boulder, Colo.: Westview Press, 1977. One of the best surveys of the arrival and settlement process of the Vietnamese in America.
—*Vietnamese Americans/history/general.*

Lim, Catherine. *Little Ironies: Stories of Singapore.* Exeter, N.H.: Heinemann Educational Books, 1978. Probably the best collection of short stories by the finest writer in Singapore.
—*Southeast Asia/literature/general.*

Nguyen, Du. *The Tale of Kieu.* Translated by Huynh Sanh Thong. New York: Random House, Vintage Books, 1973. A classic of Vietnamese literature, this long narrative poem tells the story of a beautiful, talented, well-born girl who sells herself as a concubine to save her family, is betrayed into becoming a prostitute and yet maintains her sense of honor until the end when she is reunited with her betrothed.
—*Southeast Asia/literature/general.*

Nguyen, Khac Khan. *An Introduction to Vietnamese Culture.* Tokyo: Center for East Asian Cultural Studies, 1967. Gives good background information on Vietnamese civilization.
—*Southeast Asia/history/general.*

Osborne, Milton. *Southeast Asia: An Introductory History*, rev. ed. Boston: Allen and Unwin, 1982. An authoritative introduction to the history of Southeast Asia.
—*Southeast Asia/history/general.*

The Peoples and Cultures of Cambodia, Laos, and Vietnam. Washington, D.C.: Center for Applied Linguisitics, 1981. This short, handy booklet gives a general idea of the various cultures of Indochina. Intended originally for those who were assisting with the refugees from Southeast Asia.
—*Southeast Asia/culture/general.*

Rutledge, Paul. *The Role of Religion in Ethnic Self-Identity: A Vietnamese Community.* Lanham, Md.: University Press of America, 1985. A study of the ethnic identity of Vietnamese Americans of Oklahoma City.
—*Vietnamese Americans/sociology/general.*

Sully, Francois, ed. *We the Vietnamese: Voices from Vietnam*. New York: Praeger, 1971. A collection of writings on Vietnamese civilization. Good background information.
—*Southeast Asia/history/general.*

"Vietnam: A Teacher's Guide." in *Focus on Asian Studies*. New York: The Asia Society, 1983. This guide contains five chapters, which deal briefly with the recent situation in Vietnam beginning with the French presence there and ending with the U.S. withdrawal. Each chapter answers the *what, who, when, why,* and *where* of each situation. Each chapter also has suggested classroom activities. A useful issue. Also has a resource chapter which lists books, films, and other sources.
—*Southeast Asia/History/secondary.*

Wain, Barry. *The Refused: The Agony of the Indochinese Refugee*. New York: Simon and Schuster, 1982. Describes the plight of well over 1,000,000 Indochinese refugees who left their homelands since 1975 and were rejected by their own governments, by their neighboring countries, and initially by the Western countries and Japan. Also examines the factor that led to the exodus, the profit motive of Hanoi, and an international community that was unprepared or unwilling to help resolve the crisis.
—*Southeast Asian Americans/culture/general.*

Wartski, Maureen Crane. *A Long Way From Home*. Philadelphia: Westminster Press, 1980. The story of three Vietnamese children Mai, Loc, and Kien and their adjustment to American life, especially for Kien who seemed to be constantly running into trouble. He finally realizes that he must face up to his problems instead of running away from them.
—*Vietnamese Americans/literature/intermediate.*

Whitmore, John K., ed. *An Introduction to Indochinese History, Culture, Language and Life*. Ann Arbor: Center for South and Southeast Asian Studies, University of Michigan, 1979. A good general introduction to the history and people of Vietnam, Laos, and Cambodia.
—*Southeast Asia/history/general.*

Ethnic Studies, Intercultural Relations, and General Reference Works

This section is divided into Ethnic Studies, Intercultural Relations, and General Reference Works. The reason for including sections on ethnic studies and intercultural relations is that increasingly Asian Americans are realizing that they are not along in their struggle for justice and equality nor are they unique. Other minorities have faced and continue to face similar patterns of prejudice and discrimination. Therefore, it is necessary for Asian Americans to look at the experience of other groups, such as the Blacks, Jews, Irish, and Hispanics in order to put their experiences in a broader perspective.

James A. Banks, *Teaching Ethnic Studies: Concepts and Strategies* is an excellent work that argues for the urgent need to teach ethnic studies and how to go about this. Nathan Glazer's two recent works *Ethnic Dilemmas* and *Clamor at the Gates: The New American Immigration* address the problems facing the United States as more non-Western immigrants enter the country. Another recent seminal work on race relations in the United States is a book by Benjamin B. Ringer called *"We the People" and Others: Duality and America's Treatment of its Racial Minorities*. The most comprehensive general bibliographical work on Asian Americans is *Asians in America: A Selected Annotated Bibliography* published by the Asian American Studies program at the University of California, Davis. The most recent research tool on Asian American history is the *Dictionary of Asian American History*, edited by Hyung-chan Kim.

ETHNIC STUDIES

*Allen, Leslie. *Liberty: The Statue and the American Dream*. New York: Statue of Liberty-Ellis Island Foundation, 1985. This is the official book for the centennial of the Statue of Liberty in 1986. Gives a general view of the history of immigration to this country, including Asian immigrants. Many photographs and cartoons. A good introduction. An important work.
— *Ethnic studies/history/general.*
Banks, James A., ed. *Teaching Ethnic Studies: Concepts and Strategies*. (For full citation, see Asia and Asian Americans.)
Banks, James A. *Teaching Strategies for Social Studies: Inquiry, Valuing and Decision Making*. Reading, Mass.: Addison-Wesley, 1973. This general meth-

ods text provides a conceptual framework that will help the teacher to integrate ethnic content into the regular social studies curriculum. The book is designed for use by teachers in the elementary and junior high school grades. Includes illustrations.
—*Ethnic studies/general.*

Glazer, Nathan. *Ethnic Dilemmas, 1964-1982.* Cambridge: Harvard University Press, 1983. Addresses the increasingly complex question of ethnic relations in the United States as more and more immigrants with non-Western cultural backgrounds enter the country.
—*Ethnic studies/general.*

Glazer, Nathan and Daniel Patrick Moynihan. *Beyond the Melting Pot: The Negroes, Puerto Ricans, Jews, Italians, and Irish of New York City.* 2nd ed.. Cambridge: M.I.T. Press, 1970. A classic study of minority groups of New York City based on sociological studies done during the early 1960s. The authors attacked the "melting pot" theory of assimilation by demonstrating that it did not happen, even after three or four generations.
—*Ethnic studies/history/general.*

Glazer, Nathan, ed. *Clamor at the Gates: The New American Immigration.* San Francisco: ICS Press, 1985. A collection of essays by leading authorities on the problems and history of immigration into the United States in recent years. Deals with the political and economic aspects and matters of government policy.
—*Ethnic studies/general.*

Handlin, Oscar. *The Uprooted,* 2nd ed. Boston: Little, Brown & Co., 1973. The Pulitzer Prize-winning volume on "the epic story of the great migrations that made the American People." A landmark work that not only deals with the facts but also the hearts and souls of the new immigrants. The pages are charged with feeling and poetry.
—*Ethnic studies/history/general.*

Kitano, Harry and Roger Daniels. *American Racism.* New York: Prentice-Hall, 1970. A valuable sociological and historical introduction to anti-Asian racism.
—*Ethnic studies/general.*

Reimers, David M. *Still the Open Door: The Third World Comes to America.* New York: Columbia University Press, 1985. Charts new emigration and immigration patterns in the United States since the repeal of the Chinese Exclusion Act in 1943. The major emphasis is on the post-1965 period.
—*Ethnic studies/history/general.*

Ringer, Benjamin B. *"We The People" and Others: Duality and America's Treatment of its Racial Minorities.* New York: Tavistock, 1983. A profound study of racial relations in the United States, which challenges the basic assumption that American society was "conceived in liberty and dedicated to the proposition that all men are created equal." It presents a fresh and penetrating analysis in terms of a duality, which arose out of the processes of colonization, between a "Plural Society" for nonwhites

and a "People's Domain" for whites. Four racial minorities are examined using this theoretical framework: Blacks, Chinese, Japanese, and Puerto Ricans. An extremely valuable and timely contribution to the study of the political, legal, cultural, and social aspects of racial relations.
—*Ethnic studies/history/general.*

Rose, Peter I. *They and We: Race and Ethnic Relations in the United States.* New York: Random House, 1981. A good introduction to race, ethnicity, and social status in America, which can be read with understanding by high school students. The author's distinction between prejudice and discrimination is especially useful.
—*Ethnic studies/general/secondary.*

Sowell, Thomas. *Ethnic America: A History.* New York: Basic Books, 1981. An authoritative book on ethnic groups in America with specific chapters on the Chinese and Japanese along with good comparisons with European immigrant groups.
—*Ethnic studies/history/general.*

Takaki, Ronald T., ed. *From Different Shores: Perspectives on Race and Ethnicity in America.* New York: Oxford University Press, 1987. A collection of essays on race relations in America edited by a leading Japanese American historian on Asian American history.
—*Ethnic studies/history/general.*

Takaki, Ronald T. *Iron Cages: Race and Culture in 19th-Century America* New York: Alfred A. Knopf, 1979. A comparative study of race relations in the United States. The oppression of Asians, the Chinese in particular, is analyzed in relationship to Blacks, Indians, and Mexicans. American racism is seen in the total structure of American society.
—*Ethnic studies/history/general.*

*Thernstrom, Stephan, ed. *The Harvard Encyclopedia of American Ethnic Groups.* Cambridge, Mass.: Belknap Press of Harvard University Press, 1980. This comprehensive reference work is the starting place for any research about ethnic groups in the United States. Chapters on Chinese, Japanese, Filipinos, Koreans, and Indochinese, and theme chapters on topics such as family patterns, language maintenance, and religion. Essential. Highly recommended.
—*Ethnic studies/general.*

Wheeler, Thomas C., ed. *The Immigrant Experience: The Anguish of Becoming American.* New York: Penguin Books, 1984. Nine immigrants, all talented writers, from various parts of the world, including Asia, describe the cost andpain of becoming Americans. These nine original essays and biographies were written especially for this volume. Highly personal accounts, extraordinary self-revelation. Included are the Irish, Black, Jewish, Chinese, Polish, Norwegian, English, and Italian experience. The essays show that each must pay a price and make sacrifices to become an American, and sometimes the cost has been high.
—*Ethnic studies/history/general.*

INTERCULTURAL RELATIONS

Batchelder, Donald and Elizabeth G. Warner, eds. *Beyond Experience: The Experimential Approach to Cross-Cultural Education.* Brattleboro, Vt.: Experiment Press, 1977. A collection of essays on cross-cultural education dealing with theoretical issues and practical exercises. An excellent handbook for the cross-cultural trainer and for teachers who must work with children from different cultures. Also teaches one to be aware of one's own cultural biases.
—*Intercultural/reference/general.*

Gastron, Jan. *Cultural Awareness Teaching Teaching Techniques.* Brattleboro, Vt.: Pro Lingua Associates, 1984. An excellent practical handbook for teaching cultural awareness, respect for one's own culture and other cultures. The 20 exercises are clearly explained and written with the teacher in mind.
—*Intercultural/reference/general/teacher.*

Hoopes, David S. and Paul Ventura, eds. *Intercultural Sourcebook: Cross-cultural Training Methodologies.* Yarmouth, Me.: Intercultural Press, 1979. A book strong on methodologies on cross-cultural training. Meant for trainers and useful for teachers wanting to strengthen cultural awareness amd self-awareness.
—*Intercultural/reference/general/teachers.*

Penfield, Joyce, M. Eileen Hansen, and Christine Mildner. *When Cultures Meet Face to Face: The Intercultural Experience..* New Brunswick, N.J.: Rutgers University Publications, 1986. A training package consisting of a manual and videotape for use primarily on college and university campuses. But the manual may be used separately as a useful guide for teachers and trainers. It describes activities, authentic encounters in intercultural interactions, and cultural adjustment on campus. Also has a useful annotated bibiography.
—*Intercultural/reference/general/teacher/trainer.*

Weeks, Williams H., Paul B. Peterson, and Richard Brislin, eds. *A Manual of Structured Experiences for Cross-cultural Learning.* Yarmouth, Me.: Intercultural Press, 1985. Fifty-nine structured activities with emphasis on values, feelings, and concrete incidents. Field-tested activities, fairly extensive and elaborate. Limited usefulness for the classroom.
—*Intercultural/trainers.*

REFERENCE WORKS

Ackerman, Jean Marie. *Films of a Changing World: A Critical International Guide.* Washington, D.C.: Society for International Development, 1972. An international guide to educational films made throughout the world.
—*Reference/general.*

All-Asia Guide, 12th ed. Rutland, Vt.: Charles E. Tuttle, 1982. An all-Asia travel guide arranged by country. Each section has background history, maps, information about passports, currency, language, climate, etc.
   —*Asia/reference/general.*
Anderson, G.L. *Asian Literature in English: A Guide to Information Sources.* Detroit: Gale Research Co., 1981. This guide, excellent for library use, is organized by country for easy reference. There are bibliographies for each country and region.
   —*Asia/reference/general.*
Asian American Librarians Caucus. *Asian Americans: An Annotated Bibliography for Public Libraries.* Chicago, Ill.: American Library Association, 1977. This annotated list of books on Asian Americans is divided into five sections dealing with Asian Americans in general, Chinese Americans, Japanese Americans, Korean Americans, and Filipino Americans.
   —*Asian Americans/reference.*
Asian American Materials. (catalog). (For full citation, see Asia and Asian Americans.)
Asians in America: A Selected Annotated Bibliography. (For full citation, see Asia and Asian mericans.)
A Bibliography of Asian and Asian American Books for Elementary School Youngsters. (For full citation, see Asia and Asian Americans.)
Bronner, Elizabeth H. *A Storyteller's Guide to Asian Folktales.* (For full citation, see Asia and Asian Americans.)
Bullard, Betty M. *Asia in New York City: A Guide.* (For full citation, see Asia and Asian Americans.)
China in the Classroom: Resource Catalog 1987. (For full citation, see China and Chinese Americans.)
China Resources: A Guide for the Classroom. (For full citation, see China and Chinese Americans.)
Chu, Bernice ed. *The Asian American Media Reference Guide.* (For full citation, see Asia and Asian Americans.)
Cogan, John J. and Donald O. Schneider, ed. *Perspectives on Japan: A Guide for Teachers.* (For full citation, see Japan and Japanese Americans.)
Dunn, Lynn P. *Asian Americans: A Study Guide and Sourcebook.* (For full citation, see Asia and Asian Americans.)
Focus on Asian Studies. New York: Asia Society, Inc., 1980- . An excellent source for the most recent publications on Asia, Asian Studies, and Asian American studies. Dedicated to deepening American understanding of Asia. Articles and essays are written from the pedagogical viewpoint for use by teachers in the schools. An excellent teaching aid.
   —*Asia/reference/general/teachers.*
Gentzler, J. Mason. *A Syllabus of Chinese Civilization*, 2nd ed. (For full citation, see China and Chinese Americans.)
"India. A Teacher's Guide," in *Focus on Asian Studies*, (For full citation, see Intermediate Section.)

*Kim, Hyung-chan, ed. *Dictionary of Asian American History.* (For full citation, see Asia and Asian Americans.)

Lacey, Richard. *Seeing with Feeling: Film in the Classroom.* Philadelphia: W.B.Saunders, 1972. A guide to the use of films in the classroom. —*Reference/general.*

Lanasa, Philip. *A Handbook of Activities and Resources for Teaching About Asian Americans in the Elementary School.* Third ed. Lexington, Mass.: Ginn Custom Publishing, 1983. Designed to provide better understanding among students belonging to non-Asian ethnic groups about the culture and heritage of their Asian American classmates. The book has chapters on Vietnam, Philippines, Japan, India, Korea, China, and the "self." Many activities are included in each chapter about the country, language, holidays and festivals, music, foods, and children's games, and concludes with a short bibliography. —*Asian Americans/primary/reference.*

Makino, Yasuko. *Japan Through Children's Literature: A Critical Bibliography.* (For full citation, see Japan and Japanese Americans.)

Maring, Ester G. and Joel M. *Historical and Cultural Dictionary of the Philippines.* (For full citation, see The Philippines and Filipino Americans.)

Moy, Peter. *An Annotated List of Selected Resources for Promoting and Developing an Understanding of Asian Americans.* (For full citation, see Asia and Asian Americans.)

Penfield, Joyce, M. Eileen Hansen, and Christine Mildner. *When Cultures Meet Face to Face: The Intercultural Experience.* New Brunswick, N.J.: Rutgers University Publications, 1986. A training package consisting of a manual and videotape for use primarily on college and university campuses. The manual may be used separately as a useful guide for teachers and trainers. It describes activities, authentic encounters in intercultural interactions, and cultural adjustment on campus. Also has a useful annotated bibiography. —*Intercultural/teacher/trainer.*

Sive, Mary Robinson. *China: A Multimedia Guide.* (For full citation, see China and Chinese Americans.)

Teaching About China: People and Daily Life. (For full citation, see China and Chinese Americans.)

Teaching About China: Cultural Expressions. (For full citations, see China and Chinese Americans.)

*Thernstrom, Stephan, ed. *The Harvard Encyclopedia of American Ethnic Groups.* (For full citation, see Southeast Asia and Southeast Asian Americans.)

"Vietnam: A Teacher's Guide," in *Focus on Asian Studies.* (For full citation, see Southeast Asia and Southeast Asian Americans.)

Wang, Helen. *China and Chinese Culture: A Selected Booklist to Promote a Better Understanding Grades K-8.* Bethesda, Md.: Greater Mid-Atlantic Chapter of the Chinese American Librarians Association, 1990. A most recent compilation of recent children's and young adults' books on China. The booklist is in five parts: picture books, folktales, fables and myths, nonfiction, biography, and fiction. A short section on Chinese Americans is included under nonfiction.

—*China/reference/general.*

Weeks, Williams H., Paul B. Peterson, and Richard Brislin, eds. *A Manual of Structured Experiences for Cross-Cultrual Learning.* (For full citation, see Intercultural Relations.)

Wong, Patricia M.Y. *Asian and Asian American Picture Books: A Selected Annotated Bibliography.* (For full citation, see Asia and Asian Americans.)

Part V

Appendixes and Index

Appendix A

CHRONOLOGY OF ASIANS IN AMERICA

This chronology provides a quick history of Asian immigration to America, some of the important dates and significant events, record of achievements, patterns of discrimination against Asians, and attempts to correct these wrongs. It is based on historical summaries compiled by Dr. Bob H. Suzuki, The Amherst Asian American Education Committee, P.O. Box 370, Amherst, Mass. 01059; the Asian and Pacific American Federal Employee Council, P.O. Box 7809, Ben Franklin Station, Washington, D.C. 20044; and Hyung-chan Kim, *Dictionary of Asian American History*, pp. 579-602. The following chronology of legislation was drawn from the same sources.

1761	Filipinos, impressed into the Manilla Galleon Trade (1565-1815) between Mexico and the Philippines, settle in Louisiana after jumping ship.
1784	*Empress of China*, first China clipper ship to touch China, anchors at Canton.
1785	Three Chinese crewmen—Asing, Achyun, and Accun—are stranded in Baltimore. They lived for more than a year on public funds in care of Levi Hollingsworth.
1786	George Washington appoints Major Samuel Shaw as the first American Consul to China. His primary function was to promote trade. He was responsible for the great boom in the export of Chinese porcelain.
1820	First Asian Indian arrives in America. U.S. Immigration Commission reports arrival of first Chinese to United States.
1830	First census indicates three Chinese live in United States.
1843	Nakahama Manjiro (1827-1898), shipwrecked by a typhoon, is rescued by Captain William Whitfield, who brings him to New Bedford, Massachusetts.
1847	The first group of three Chinese students, including Yung Wing (1828-1912), arrives to study in the United States.
1848	Gold strike at Sutter's Mill, California draws Chinese immigrants to the West Coast. This is the most important event that brought the Chinese to America. The bulk of Chinese immigrants came soon thereafter to work on the railroads, in mines, fisheries, farms, orchards, canneries, garment industries, manufacturing of cigars, boots, etc.
1850	California's Foreign Miners' Tax (see Legislation). Hamada Hikozo (1837-1897) is rescued by an American sailing ship. He is educated and becomes the first American citizen of Japanese ancestry.

1859   Exclusion of Chinese from public schools in San Francisco.

1860   Census records that there are 34,933 Chinese living in the United States.

1865   Chinese are recruited to work on the Transcontinental Railroad. At its peak more than 10,000 Chinese worked for the Central Pacific R.R. Co.

1867   Fukuzawa Yukichi (1835-1901), educator and author, visits the United States. He is mainly responsible for the introduction of Japan to the Western world.

1868   Japanese contract workers arrive in Hawaii to work on the sugar plantations, but when the Japanese government learns of maltreatment of these workers, Japanese emigration stops for the next 17 years.
            The United States and China sign the Burlingame Treaty, which recognizes the right of Chinese to immigrate for "purposes of curiosity, trade, or permanent residence," but expressly restricts the right of naturalization.

1869   Transcontinental Railroad is completed. Predominantly Chinese laborers built most of the western section. Approximately 15,000 Chinese workers are temporarily unemployed.
            First Japanese settlers arrive in Gold Hill, California. They found the Wakamatsu Tea and Silk Farm Colony under the leadership of John Henry Schnell.

1871   Anti-Chinese riots break out in Los Angeles and other cities.

1872   The Iwakura Mission led by Prince Iwakura arrives in the United States with 53 Japanese students who are left behind to study in the United States.

1872   The Chinese Education Mission, organized and led by Yung Wing, arrives in the United States with 30 Chinese students to study in the United States.

1877   Denis Kearney helps organize the Workingmen's Party of California and becomes its leader. Famed for his slogan "All Chinese Must Go!" he demands the exclusion of Chinese immigration, claiming that the Chinese deprives Americans of decent jobs.

1870s   Nationwide recession causes West Coast labor problems. "Cheap Chinese labor" becomes the scapegoat. Mobs destroy Chinese communities in many areas of California and elsewhere. Bloodshed and riots become everyday occurrences in San Francisco.

1879   Sun Yat-sen (1866-1925), founder of the Republic of China, arrives in Hawaii.

1880   Anti-Chinese riots break out in Denver, Colorado.

1880   Between 1871-1880, 149 Japanese immigrate to the United States according to U.S. Census Bureau.

1882   Chinese Exclusion Act (see Legislation).

1883   Korean diplomatic mission led by Prince Min Yong-ik arrives in San Francisco.

1885	The first shipload of Japanese workers arrives in Honolulu, Hawaii. This is the beginning of large-scale immigration of Japanese to Hawaii.
1885	Anti-Chinese riots break out in Rock Springs, Wyoming.
1886	Japan lifts ban restricting emigration of Japanese.
1886	Anti-Chinese riots break out in Seattle, WA.
1888	Scott Act (see Legislation).
1890	According to the U.S. Census Bureau there are 107,488 Chinese in the United States.
1892	Geary Act (see Legislation).
1893	Swami Vivekananda speaks at the Parliament of Religions at the World's Columbian Exposition in Chicago.
1895	Mr. Bungara, a Parsee, brings Indian brass to California.
1898	The United States acquires the Philippines from Spain, which formally ends the Spanish-American War. Hawaii is annexed by the United States, along with 31,000 Filipino laborers.
1900	25,000 Japanese live in America. Between 1900-1910 almost 5,000 Sikhs emigrate to America because of a severe drought in the Punjab region.
1900	The Japanese Association of America is formed to fight racial discrimination.
1900	Hawaii becomes a territory of the United States.
1902	Congress indefinitely extends the prohibition against Chinese immigration and the denial of naturalization.
1903	Korean contract laborers arrive in Hawaii, marking beginning of Korean immigration to the U.S.
1905	Japan occupies Korea as part of the settlement of the Russo-Japanese War and halts Korean immigration to Hawaii.
1906	The San Francisco School Board passes a resolution whereby all Korean, Chinese, and Japanese children are sent to the segregated Oriental Public Schools on the south side of Clay Street. The order is rescinded after vigorous protest.
1907	President Theodore Roosevelt enters into "Gentlemen's Agreement" with Japan to restrict Japanese immigration to mainland United States and Hawaii. As a result, single Filipino men are recruited to work in the fisheries of Alaska and the growing agri-businesses of Hawaii and California.
1910	Angel Island is set up as a detention center for non-laboring Asians seeking entry into the United States. Long waiting periods under sub-human conditions cause suicides on Angel Island. Beginning of large-scale immigration of Korean laborers, picture brides, and political refugees to the United States.
1910	Syngman Rhee returns to Korea after receiving his Ph.D. from Princeton.
1913	Eleven Korean apricot pickers are driven out of Hemet, California.

1913	California Alien Land Acts (see Legislation).
1914	Dr. S.G. Pandit becomes a U.S. citizen by claiming that he was white, but nine years later the government tries to cancel his certificate of naturalization.
1919	Korean independence movement at its height. Koreans in the United States protest Japanese occupation of Korea.
1921	Chinese women marrying American citizens cannot automatically become citizen.
1922	Ozawa case (see Legislation).
	Cable Act (see Legislation).
1923	Court ruling on definition of "Caucasian" set off proceedings by the U.S. government to deny citizenship to 70 Asian Indians who had already been naturalized in the previous 15 years. From this time onward until 1946 Asian Indians were denied U.S. citizenship and rights to own property in the United States.
1924	Quota Immigration Act (see Legislation).
1927	Anti-Asian attacks and riots occur during the Great Depression, especially against Filipinos who are concentrated in agriculture as stoop laborers.
1934	Tydings-McDuffey Act (see Legislation).
1937	Chinese Americans protest Japanese invasion of China.
1939	Koreans in Los Angeles demonstrate against U.S. scrap iron and airplane fuel shipment to Japan.
1941.	The United States enters World War II as a result of the Japanese attack on Pearl Harbor. Incident erupts in vigilante violence against the Japanese.
	A third of the Filipinos in the United States enlist to fight against the Japanese who invaded the Philippines.
1942	Executive Order 9066 (see Legislation).
1943	Magnuson Act (see Legislation).
	Secretary of War Stimson permits the creation of all-Nisei (second-generation Japanese Americans) unit, the 100th Battalion. This all-Nisei unit is incorporated into the 442 regimental combat team.
1945	War Brides Act removes racial restriction for Asian brides and permits their entry to the United States. Many Japanese war brides migrate to United States. Six thousand Chinese women enter the United States as war brides.
1946	The Philippines becomes independent. U.S. citizenship is offered to all Filipinos in the country.
	Luce-Celler Bill (see Legislation).
1947	India declares independence.
	From 1947-1957 approximately 2,500 Indians and Pakistanis come to the United States.
1948	Evacuation Claims Act (see Legislation).
	Interracial marriage (see Legislation).

Filipino-American Vicki Manalo Draves becomes the first woman ever in Olympic history to win both the high- and low-diving gold medals during the London Olympics.

1949   The United States breaks off diplomatic ties with the newly formed People's Republic of China.

1952   McCarran-Walter Act (see Legislation).
       Japanese American Tommy Kono wins the Olympic gold medal for weightlifting-lightweight division.

1950s Korean War breaks out, resulting in the immigration of Korean war brides.

1955   Filipinos are the second fastest growing ethnic group in the United States, but they also register a very low average income.

1956   Dr. Dalip Sing Saund is elected to the House of Representatives.

1957   Nobel Prizes in physics are awarded to Chinese American physicists Chen-ning Yang and Tsung-dao Lee.

1959   "Confession Period" for Chinese immigrants who cooperate with the authorities by informing on other illegal aliens.
       Daniel Inouye becomes the first Japanese American representative in Congress.
       Hiram Fong becomes the first Chinese American senator.

1965   The Immigration Act (see Legislation).
       Beginning of rapid increase of Korean immigration to the United States results eventually in the emergence of Koreatowns in Los Angeles and Chicago.

1968   Third World Strike begins at San Francisco State College and spreads to University of California, Berkeley in 1969. These activities result in the establishment of Asian American studies programs at various universities throughout the country.

1971   Martial Law in South Korea increases Korean immigration to the United States.

1972   Martial Law in the Philippines increases Filipino immigration to the United States.

1975   The fall of Vietnam and Cambodia stimulates large-scale immigration into the United States of refugees from Vietnam, Cambodia, and Laos.
       In May the Indochina Migration and Refugee Assistance Act admits 130,000 refugees, mostly Vietnamese but includes Cambodians and Laotians as well.

1976   Chinese American Samuel Ting wins the Nobel Prize for Physics.
       Eduardo Manlapit becomes the first Filipino American county executive in the United States, serving as Mayor of Kauai.

1979   First official recognition for Asian and Pacific Americans Heritage Week, May 4-10 by President Jimmy Carter.
       Normalization of relations between the People's Republic of China and the United States of America.

1980   Asian and Pacific Americans, according to the U.S. Census Bureau, number 3.5 million or 1.5% of total U.S. population—doubling the official 1970 figures.

President Jimmy Carter establishes seven-member Commission on Wartime Relocation and Internment of Civilians to study longlasting effects of Executive Order 9066.

1981   120,000 refugees from Southeast Asia enter the United States.

Ku Klux Klan (KKK) of Texas burns boats, symbolizing their opposition to Vietnamese immigration and programs.

1982   Reagan administration establishes a ceiling of 100,000 Southeast Asian refugee admissions.

1984   Japanese American Ellison Onizakakis becomes the first Asian American to fly in the space shuttle.

1986   Three Chinese Americans, Wang An, I.M. Pei, and Franklin Chang, receive the Liberty Medal at the centennial celebration of the Statue of Liberty.

1988   Redress Bill (see Legislation).

Appendix B

LEGISLATION REGARDING ASIANS

1850   California passes a monthly Foreign Miners' License Tax to discourage Chinese miners. All foreign miners must pay $20 per month. For 20 years, before the law was repealed in 1870, the Chinese miners paid 98 percent of the $1.5 million collected through this tax.

1854   The California State Supreme Court rules that the Chinese are included in an 1849 law, which provided that "no Black, or Mulatto person, or Indian, shall be allowed to give evidence in favor of, or against, a white man."

1855   The California Legislature passes an act, which requires the owner of a vessel to pay $50 tax for each passenger not eligible for citizenship. This law was directed at restricting the socio-economic activity of the Chinese in California. Declared illegal in 1857.

1860   A California law is passed, which levies a $4 per month tax against Chinese engaged in fishing.

1860   A California statute excludes Chinese, Indians, and blacks from public schools.

1862   The California Legislature passes a police tax, which requires a Chinese in the state to pay $2.50 if he has not paid the Foreign Miners' License Tax.
California legislature passes an act to protect free white labor against Chinese coolie labor and discourages the immigration of Chinese into California.

1867   Federal district court declares Chinese ineligible for citizenship.

1870   A "Cubic Air" ordinance of San Francisco Board of Supervisors makes it mandatory for a lodging house to provide at least 500 cubic feet of clean air for each adult person in his or her apartment. At first it is applied generally, but by 1873 it remained in force only in the crowded Chinese section of San Francisco. Because of the living conditions of the Chinese, this was an impossible law to obey. As a result many Chinese were arrested.

1870   Any person bringing a Chinese or Japanese to California without evidence of the immigrant's good character will be penalized with not less than $1,000 nor more than $5,000 fine or face imprisonment.

1873   Laundry Tax. All laundries that did not use horse-drawn vehicles had to pay $15 every three months for a license. Since the Chinese did not use vehicles but carried goods on a pole on their shoulders, they had to pay the tax.

1876	"Queue Ordinance" of the City of County of San Francisco states that every Chinese prisoner in jail would have to have his hair cut within one inch of his scalp.
1879	California adopts a new Constitution, which contains many discriminatory measures against the Chinese: 1) Chinese immigrants are denied naturalization; 2) corporations cannot hire Chinese; 3) Chinese are denied employment in any municipal, county or state public works except in the punishment of crime; 4) coolie trade is illegal; and 5) the legislature can remove Chinese to regions beyond the limits of cities and towns.
1881	California Governor George C. Parkins proclaims March 4th as a legal holiday for anti-Chinese demonstrations.
1882	Congress passes the Chinese Exclusion Act, stopping Chinese immigration for a ten-year period. When the first law expired in 1892, it was renewed for another ten years. Then in 1902 and 1904, Congress passed new laws which, in effect, put Chinese exclusion on a permanent basis. The Chinese Exclusion Act was finally repealed in 1943.
1888	The Scott Act, passed by Congress, prohibits re-entry of Chinese laborers who leave the United States for temporary visits to China (permitted under the Exclusion Act). Some 20,000 certificates of re-entry are declared null and void.
1892	The Geary Act, passed by Congress, extends the Chinese Exclusion Act for another ten years. Requires certificates of residence for all Chinese laborers or else they will be deported.
1898	After the annexation of Hawaii, Congress passes a joint resolution prohibiting further immigration of Chinese into Hawaii. And those Chinese already in Hawaii cannot come to the mainland United States.
1902	The Chinese Exclusion Act of 1882 is extended indefinitely by the United States Congress.
1913	The California legislature passes the Alien Land Acts, which prohibit aliens who are ineligible for citizenship (Chinese, Japanese, and Korean) from owning or leasing property.
1922	Congress passes the Cable Act, which denies U.S. citizenship of a woman who marries an alien ineligible for U.S. citizenship. Specifically, U.S.-born Chinese American women marrying foreign-born Asians automatically lose their citizenship. However, they could regain it through naturalization.
1922	In the *Ozawa* case, the U.S. Supreme Court declares that Japanese immigrants cannot become naturalized citizens.
1923	In the Bhagat Singh Thind case, the U.S. Supreme Court rules that Asian Indians are not eligible for U.S. citizenship.

1924   National Origins Act, known to Asians as the Asian Exclusion Act, excludes the immigration of all Asian laborers. Under this act, alien wives of American citizens are not allowed entry into the United States if the wives are ineligible for citizenship. Only students aspiring for master's degrees can enter the United States.

1925   Legislative Act specifies that Filipinos are ineligible for citizenship unless they serve three years in the American Navy.

1934   Tydings-McDuffey Act prohibits the immigration of Filipinos to the United States. It declares the Philippines a commonwealth and guarantees independence in ten years, and further limits emigration from the Philippines to 50 persons a year.

1935   The Filipino Repatriation Act provides transportation expenses for Filipinos who desire to return to the Philippines, but also stipulates that they cannot re-enter the United States.

1942   Executive Order 9066, signed by President Roosevelt, authorizes the establishment of military areas and evacuation of civilians from these areas. This action is responsible for the removal and relocation of more than 110,000 persons of Japanese ancestry.

1943   Congress passes the Magnuson Act, which finally repeals the Chinese Exclusion Act of 1882. This law allows Chinese to become naturalized citizens and gives China a quota of 105 immigrants per year.
        In *Hirabayashi v. United States*, the Supreme Court affirms the legality of Executive Order 9066.

1943   In *Korematsu v. United States*, the Supreme Court affirms correction and constitutionality of curfew provision of Executive Order 9066.

1946   The Luce-Celler Bill is signed into law. It allows Asian Indians to become U.S. citizens and establishes a quota of 100 immigrants from India to the United States per year

1948   The Displaced Persons Act is signed into law, which allows 15,000 Chinese in the United States to adjust their legal status.
        The Japanese American Evacuation Claims Act is signed into law. It permits former evacuees to file claims against the government for their financial losses during the evacuation.
        The Supreme Court declares California's law banning interracial marriage unconstitutional.

1952   The McCarran-Walter Act (Immigration and Nationality Act of 1952) repeals the National Origins Act of 1924, confers the rights of naturalization and eventual citizenship for Asians not born in the United States, and sets a quota of 105 immigrants per year for each Asian country.

1965   President Lyndon B. Johnson signs into law a landmark immigration law that not only repeals the National Origins Act (1924), but also establishes a new immigration policy enabling large numbers of immigrants from Asian countries to come to the United States. This law places immigration from Asian countries to the United States on an equal footing with European countries.

1974   In *Lau v. Nichols*, the Supreme Court rules that the failure to provide adequate education to non-English speaking students is a violation of the Equal Protection Clause of the Constitution, and declares that bilingual education has to be provided to non-English speaking students.

1975   The Indochina Migration and Refugee Assistance Act is passed to provide funds for resettlement programs.

1976   The Indochinese Refugee Children's Assistance Act is passed to provide funds for the education of children from Vietnam, Kampuchea, and Laos.

1976   Executive Order 9066 (1942), responsible for the relocation of Japanese during World War II, is officially rescinded.

1983   Congressional Committee issues report critical of incarceration of 110,000 Japanese Americans during World War II.

1988   Congress passes "Redress Bill" that promises payment of $20,000 to each survivor of the internment camps and apologizes to the Japanese who had been wrongly incarcerated during World War II.

Appendix C

LETTER TO CONFERENCE PARTICIPANTS

Dear Participants:

As the dates of the conference (June 20-23) approach, may I ask you to take a few minutes from your busy schedule to look over this questionnaire. We would like to draw upon your expertise to help us focus attention on some key issues, values, and concepts concerning Asian Americans for discussion at the conference and to stimulate our thinking.

It is the purpose of this survey also to gather and assess the opinions and responses of both Asians and non-Asians that would help to dispel stereotypes and misperceptions and promote true understanding between Asian Americans and the non-Asian American community. The results of the survey will be incorporated into a handbook for teachers and other professionals concerned with Asian Americans.

In order to explore the various facets of the Asian American experience from diverse perspectives, the design of this survey is purposely broad in scope and focus. It is important that we have a wide range of responses from social scientists, educators, as well as humanists, including writers, critics, film makers, playwrights, and doctors, engineers, and members of the business community. Because of your expressed interest and personal experience in working with Asian Americans, we are especially eager to learn about your views and to increase your input and participation in the conference.

The questionnaire will take about 30 minutes to fill out, and all the information will be kept strictly confidential and anonymous. The data will be computerized and analyzed on a group basis. Even if you are not able to attend the conference, we would also appreciate your returning the questionnaire since your input will be important for the survey and conference.

We appreciate your participation and concern. Please return the completed survey in the enclosed and addressed envelope.

Sincerely,

Peter Li
Conference Chair

Please return questionaire to: ECAAEC Survey
                                 International Center
                                 Rutgers University
                                 180 College Avenue
                                 NewBrunswick, NJ 08903

PERCEPTIONS REGARDING ASIAN AMERICANS

I. Stereotypes (which may be positive, negative or neutral) and
    Misperceptions

1. What do you think are the three most common stereotypes
    non-Asians have concerning Asian Americans?

    a) _____

    b) _____

    c) _____

2. What do you think are the sources of these stereotypes?

    a) _____

    b) _____

    c) _____

3. What do you think are the three most serious misperceptions
    non-Asians have concerning Asian Americans that need to be
    clarified?

    a) _____

    b) _____

    c) _____

4. Do you have any specific suggestions as to how these misper-
    ceptions can be corrected?

    a) _____

    b) _____

    c) _____

II. Values and Communication Patterns

     Please choose one specific Asian American ethnic group that
     you are familiar with to complete this section.

     Asian American ethnic group selected: _____

1. What do you think are the three most important core cultural values of this particular Asian American group?

    a) _____

    b) _____

    c) _____

2. What would be the key phrases or adjectives that best describe this particular Asian American group in their interaction with other non-Asian groups?

    a) _____

    b) _____

    c) _____

3. Do you feel there is a <u>major</u> communication style difference between this particular Asian American group and other non-Asian groups?   No _____, Yes _____.   Little differences _____

    If yes, can you briefly explain the difference?

    _____

    _____

4. If you are in contact with members of this particular Asian American group on a regular basis, can you recall an incident from the recent past that has caused communication breakdown or conflict between a member of this particular Asian American group and the other person (or yourself)?

    a) Describe the incident briefly :

    b) Was the problem resolved? No _____, Yes _____. If yes, how did you resolve the communication problem?

5. Are there any recent problems in Asian American communities which you feel need to be identified and addressed?

a) _____

b) _____

c) _____

6. What problems do Asian-American children have in adjusting to life in the United States (e.g., 1st generation parents vs 2nd generation children)?

a) _____

b) _____

c) _____

7. Name some ways in which the adjustment of these Asian-American children affect family life?

a) _____

b) _____

c) _____

8. What do you perceive as the major intercultural communication problems that face members of this particular group when communicating with other non-Asians (e.g. Blacks, Caucasians, Hispanics, Native-Americans, etc,)?

a) _____

b) _____

c) _____

9. What do you perceive as the major intercultural communication problems that face members of this particular group when communicating with members of other Asian groups?

a) _____

b) _____

c) _____

10. If a curriculum handbook for teachers were developed, what key terms would you include in the glossary that would be helpful for understanding Asian Americans?

a) _____

b) _____

c) _____

III. Instructional Setting

1. If you were to implement the ideal Asian American course in the school curriculum for the purpose of understanding Asian American experiences and cultures what would be some of the key topics you would include in your course?

   a) _____

   b) _____

   c) _____

2. Can you suggest some specific activities that have worked well in your experience?

   a) _____

   b) _____

   c) _____

3. What do you think should be the ideal characteristics or qualities of an instructor who teaches such a course?

   a) _____

   b) _____

   c) _____

4. What do you think should be the ideal background experiences of such an instructor?

   a) _____

   b) _____

   c) _____

5. If you are a teacher/instructor or Asian American profes-sional involved with Asian American activities, would you like to receive additional training to deal more effectively with Asian Americans? No _____, Yes _____.

   If yes, what kind of training would you like to receive?

   a) _____

   b) _____

   c) _____

6. Would you like to recommend two or three resources (books,

films, filmstrips, etc.) that you have found especially helpful in your work in understanding of Asian American experiences and cultures? Please document the source materials (author, title, publisher, date).

a) _____

b) _____

c) _____

7. What recommendations do you have for improving understanding of Asian Americans for which the schools can take special responsibility?

a) _____

b) _____

c) _____

8. Do you believe that Asian languages should be taught in the schools? Yes _____. No _____.

Explain your answer briefly: _____

_____

IV. Demographic Information (for statistical purpose only)
Please circle the appropriate response or fill in the blanks:

1. Sex: M   F   2. Age: _____

3. Occupation: _____

4. Language: Bilingual _____. Specify: _____

         Monolingual ____

5. Prior or present working experience with Asian Americans:

No _____, Yes _____. Length of experience_____

If Yes, briefly describe_____

_____

6. Cultural background: Asian_____. Non Asian _____

7. Specific ethnic background:_____
   (e.g. Japanese-American, Chinese American, Asian Indian, Philipino, Caucasian, etc.)

8. If you are an Asian American, what generation are you?

a) First generation immigrant _____
b) Second generation   _____
c) Third generation   _____
d) Beyond third generation _____

9. If you are an Asian, do you identify yourself primarily as
    an Asian or primarily as an American?
    a) Asian _____   b) American _____
    c) Other (please specify)_____

    Explain your answer briefly:_____

    _____

10. If you are an Asian, do you think most Americans consider
    you as primarily an Asian or primarily as American?

    a) Asian _____   b) American _____

    c) Other (please specify) _____

    Explain your answer briefly:_____

11. Finally would you prefer to be identified as
    a) Asian _____   b) Asian American _____
    c) Oriental _____   d) American Asian _____
    e) American _____   f) Other (please specify)_____

    Explain your answer briefly:_____

    _____

I will _____/will not _____ be able to attend the conference.

Thank you very much for your cooperation in filling out this
survey!

Additional remarks:_____

_____

_____

_____

_____

Contributors

Marjorie H. Li, Technical Services Librarian at Rutgers University, was born in China and raised in Taiwan, where she attended the National Taiwan University. She continued her studies at the University of Chicago with a fellowship in the field of library science. She has held various positions at Rutgers University Libraries including acting head of the East Asian Library and has been active in the Chinese American Librarians Association.

Peter Li is Associate Professor of Chinese and Director of Asian Studies at Rutgers University. Born in China and educated in the United States, he received his B.A. from the University of Washington and his Ph.D. in Chinese Literature from the University of Chicago. He is an author, contributor, and editor of books and articles on Chinese literature.

Dr. Joyce Penfield is Assistant Professor of Language Education at Rutgers University, where she prepares teachers of English as a second language, bilingual education, and foreign languages.

Dr. Abraham Resnick is a Professor of Education at Jersey City State College, New Jersey, and for many years was Director of the Instructional Materials Center at the Rutgers University Graduate School of Education. He specializes in curriculum development and has written a number of social studies books for students and teachers.

Penny Wong Sing is a member of the New Jersey Ethnic Advisory Council. She has taught numerous craft classes in New Jersey and often conducts origami workshops.

Margaret So, a native of Hong Kong, is a student of graphic arts at Rutgers University.

Stella Ting-Toomey is Associate Professor of Communication at Arizona State University, Tempe. Her primary teaching and research are in intercultural communication and interpersonal communication.

Index

Ackerman, Jean Marie, *Films of a Changing World*, 79
Alpana, 59-60
Anti-Asian legislation, 78, 173-176
Aoki, Rocky, 11
Asian American Studies Programs
  Berkeley School District, 92
  Collection development, 93-94
  Curriculum development, 93
  Fort Lee School District, 91-92
  Outreach programs, 95
Asian Americans
  Accultration, 9-10
  Admission quota, 11-12
  Alienation, 4-5
  Common concerns, 1
  Contributions, 11
  Dual allegiance, 3-4
  Generational conflicts, 2, 5-7, 26
  Idealization of America, 7
  Inability to communicate, 3, 26-27
  Involvement in politics, 11
  Misconceptions, 24, 29
  Self-rejection, 10

Bulosan, Carlos, *America is in the Heart*, 7

Calligraphy, 35-37
Carp kite, 38-39
Children's Day, 38
Chin, Frank, *The Chickencoop Chinaman*, 9
"Chinaman", 9
Chinese New Year Parade, 42-44
Chinese American Librarians Association, x
Chinese Exclusion Act, 132
Chopsticks game, 63-64

Chu, Bernice, *The Asian American Media Reference Guide*, 79
Chung, Kyung-wha, 11
Clavell, James, *Tai-pan*, 67
Cultural stereotypes, 19-21
  about Americans, 87
  Career options, 69
  Chinese American, 25
  Filipino American, 25
  In literature, 67-68
  Japanese American, 25
  Korean American, 25
  Media portrayal, 70
  Sources, 23
  Values system, 25
  Vietnamese American, 25

Daruma doll, 47
Diwali Festival, 59

East Coast Asian American Education Conference (ECAAEC), ix
  Survey, 20-21,177-183
Ethnocentrism, 81

Haiku, 50
Houston, Wakatsuki, *Farewell to Manzanar*, 3
Hwang, David Henry, *M. Butterfly*, 1

Internment, Japanese, 4-5

Jan Ken Po(Game), 40
Jianzi(Game), 45-46

Khokad(Game), 57-58
Kingston, Maxine Hong, *Woman Warrior*, 1, 2-3

Lacey, Richard, 79

Lowe, Pardee, *Father and Glorious Descendant*, 7-8

Ma, Yo Yo, 11
Mehta, Zubin, 11
"Melting pot" theory, 78
Model minority, 12

Name chop (Seal), 40-41
New Jersey Department of Higher Education, ix
Nisei, 4

Okada, John, *No-No Boy*, 5
Origami(Game), 51-52
Origami Center of America, 51
Ozawa, Seiji, 11

Pacific Asian Coalition, ix-x
Paper cutting, 53-54
Pei, I. M., xi, 11

Return of the Dragon, 70
Rohmer, Sax, *Dr. Fu Manchu*, 29
Rutgers, the State University
International Center, ix
Research Council, x

Shogun, 70

Tan, Amy, *The Joy Luck Club*, 1
Tangram Puzzle, 55-56
Ting, Samuel, 11

Wang, An, 11
Wong, Jade Snow, *Fifth Chinese Daughter*, 5-6
Wood, Jeanne Clark, 95
"Adopt-a-Student" Program, 95

Yamasaki, Yoshiro, 11